OUTLOOK 2003

MICHAEL PRICE

in
easy steps

In easy steps is an imprint of Computer Step
Southfield Road . Southam
Warwickshire CV47 0FB . United Kingdom
www.ineasysteps.com

Notice of Liability
Every effort has been made to ensure that this book contains accurate and current information. However, Computer Step and the author shall not be liable for any loss or damage suffered by readers as a result of any information contained herein.

Trademarks
Microsoft® and Windows® are registered trademarks of Microsoft Corporation. All other trademarks are acknowledged as belonging to their respective companies.

Printed and bound in the United Kingdom

ISBN 1-84078-273-0

Contents

1

2

3

4

5

6

7 Task Manager   119

8 Journal and Notes   133

Getting started with Outlook

In this chapter you will see how Outlook implements electronic mail (e-mail), personal information management (PIM), and how to set up your Internet service and e-mail, replacing any existing e-mail or PIM applications you may have.

Covers

Chapter One

Electronic mail and PIM functions

Whilst using your computer, whether for hobbies, studies, or business, you will create and send or receive information of many different types, in many different forms. You may have word processing documents and reports, electronic mail schedules and timetables, tasks to perform and people to contact. You also have access to a vast data store through the medium of the Internet. With so much information to deal with, it can be hard to remember everything that is available, and even harder to find it when you need it.

The large hard disks featured on modern PCs serve to emphasize the problem, because there is much less restriction on the type and amount of data that you can afford to keep. The range and variety of computer applications allow you to manipulate and process this information, creating even more information to manage.

If you are working with others in a formal or informal team, then you may find that you are spending most of your time searching for information that they require and preparing it in a form suitable for transferring. You may have to look in many locations to collect the information that you need.

Where Outlook fits in

In this book, the term Outlook refers to Outlook 2003 (part of Office 2003). You'll also have a copy of Outlook Express 6.0 (installed with Internet Explorer 6.0 and Windows XP). This product is used in collaboration with Outlook 2003 to provide Newsreader capabilities. It can also be used as an alternative e-mail system on systems without Office 2003.

The data you need can be spread out in many different places and different forms. Details of meetings may be written on your calendar or in your planning diary. Reports and letters may be stored on the hard disk in your PC. You may have additional information, comments, suggestions and corrections in the form of e-mail messages from others, plus a record of the e-mails that you have sent.

You may already have separate applications that help you with some of these tasks: an e-mail system to handle electronic messages, an Internet newsreader, a PC based fax system, or an electronic personal information manager such as Schedule+. These systems will each have their address book to keep details of the senders and the recipients, hence often carrying duplicated information.

You won't have to lose your existing e-mail message files or your current address book details when you upgrade your software. Outlook will migrate them for you.

Outlook is a desktop information management program that is designed as one product, to help you coordinate and manage all the different categories of data that you deal with. It uses a standard interface, and enables you to control and schedule your tasks, data, e-mail and contacts. It can even keep track of the documents you create. It provides support for Internet news, and it works with your office applications and your Internet browser.

With Outlook, you can manage personal or business information on your own stand-alone system, or as part of a group connected by a network or linked through the Internet.

In Outlook, information is organized in folders, and its activities are divided into sets of functions related to these folders. So, for example, the Inbox folder displays your messages and allows you to forward them or to send replies.

Depending on which edition of Office you use (see page 12) your version of Outlook 2003 may include the enhanced product Business Contact Manager (see page 11 and pages 164-174) in the form of an Add-in to the main application.

Features of Outlook 2003

Outlook was first released as Outlook 97, included as an integral part of Microsoft Office 97 and of Microsoft Exchange Server. As Outlook 98 it became a separate product, which introduced the trademark Outlook Bar navigation feature, and supported the full set of Outlook functions.

Functions of Outlook

- Send and receive messages
- Manage contact details (address book)
- Scheduling and diary management
- Task management and assignment
- Journal logging
- Notes storage and control

When Office 2000 was released, it included a matching Outlook 2000 which integrated e-mail into the other Office applications. Following the release of Windows XP, Office XP and the associated Outlook 2002 picked up on new features such as Smart Tags and Task Panes, and enhanced reliability. It also eliminated the distinction between corporate/workgroup and Internet mail-only modes of operation.

Outlook 2003, available stand-alone or as part of Office 2003 (see page 12) includes all these functions, and continues the evolution. It includes a major revision of the user interface, replacing the Outlook Bar with the Shortcuts Pane and the Navigation Pane.

Outlook has new features in many areas, including:

Interface
- Research Library Task Pane
- Reading Layout Mode
- Address properties available from the Reading Pane

The Reading Pane (see page 26) is the new way of providing a view of the content of new messages without having to open them.

Messaging
- Unlimited number of messages displayed in mail view
- View messages by category
- Search folders to assist in searching for messages
- Send messages with Live attachments

Calendar and Collaboration
- Side-by-side viewing of multiple calendars
- Document workspaces
- Create a Meeting Workspace in a meeting request

Contacts
- Business Contact Manager
- Contact picture

Business Contact Manager (BCM) is a single-user COM add-in for Outlook 2003 that provides additional features for tracking contact activity and sales opportunities. See pages 164-174 for more details.

Security and Content Management
- Digital signature and Kerberos authentication
- Information Rights Management
- Junk E-Mail Filters
- Trusted Senders and Trusted Recipients Lists

Microsoft Server support
- Integration with SharePoint Portal Server
- Live Communications Server integration
- Cached exchange mode
- Intelligent Connectivity
- RPC Connectivity to Exchange via HTTP

Outlook Performance Improvements
- Incremental change synchronization
- Smart change synchronization
- Pre-synchronization reporting
- Buffer packing
- Outlook performance monitoring
- Send and Receive groups

Outlook 2003 requirements

Outlook 2003 and the other applications associated with Office 2003 will not run on the Windows Me, Windows 98, and Windows NT operating systems. If your PC is currently running one of these operating systems, you must upgrade the operating system before installing Outlook 2003.

Microsoft Windows operating system

The examples in this book assume you have Windows XP installed on your PC, but the comments and recommendations apply to PCs with Windows 2000 Professional (with service pack 3) and to later editions of Windows. Outlook 2003 and Office 2003 will not operate with earlier versions of Windows such as Windows Me and Windows 98.

Office applications

Your existing word processing, spreadsheet and other applications will exchange information with Outlook 2003. However, it is best if these applications are designed to work with Outlook 2003, like the applications in Microsoft Office 2003. Other versions and office products will also inter-operate with Outlook 2003, and allow you to import and export data and documents.

Internet service and software

You will need Internet Explorer or another Internet browser, plus any software provided by your chosen ISP (see page 14).

Version of Outlook

There are two versions of Outlook 2003, the Basic version which contains all the usual Outlook functions, and the Professional version which has some extra features, including Information Rights Management (IRM) and Arbitrary XML (allowing you to develop your own XML schema for defining information). The version you have depends on which edition of Office 2003 you have installed.

If there's a student in the house, the best value edition of Office 2003 is the Student/Teacher edition, where a single copy offers three licenses for Word, Excel, Outlook and PowerPoint.

Office 2003 Edition	Outlook version	BCM
Professional	Professional	Yes
Professional Enterprise	Professional	Yes
Small Business	Basic	Yes
Standard	Basic	No
Basic (pre-installed)	Basic	No
Student/teacher	Basic	No
Outlook 2003 stand-alone	Professional	Yes

The Business Contact Manager application is included with Outlook 2003 stand-alone and with some editions of Office 2003, but it is not available as a separate stand-alone product.

You should apply the latest service pack releases to your operating system before you install Outlook 2003.

To run this software you must have the appropriate hardware components on your PC. You'll need these items or their functional equivalent:

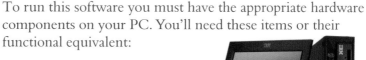

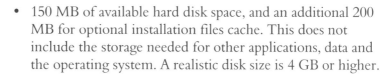

- PC with Pentium 233 MHz processor or higher. A Pentium III processor is recommended.

- For Outlook 2003 128 MB memory, or higher is recommended.

- 150 MB of available hard disk space, and an additional 200 MB for optional installation files cache. This does not include the storage needed for other applications, data and the operating system. A realistic disk size is 4 GB or higher.

- CD-ROM or DVD drive.

- Super VGA 800 x 600 or higher-resolution monitor with 256 colors or greater.

- Microsoft Mouse, Microsoft IntelliMouse or compatible pointing device.

- Data or data/fax modem – 33.3kbps or 56kbps for basic e-mail, but intensive Internet activity may require more speed, and DSL or Cable connections would be better.

You should allow about 15% of the hard disk space for the working storage needed for mail and Web browsing.

Additional items or services may be required to use certain features of Outlook. For multimedia and sound, you'll need an accelerated video card for improved graphics. For speech recognition, a Pentium II 400 MHz or higher processor is advised, plus a close-talk microphone and audio output headphones or speakers. Access to machines running Windows Server 2003 is required for Windows SharePoint Services and for IRM features.

You can use a mobile device such as a Pocket PC or an Internet enabled mobile phone to access your e-mail and your calendar. See pages 154-162 for more information.

Windows Mobile 2003

This supports a range of mobile devices, including Pocket PCs and mobile phones, and uses the Windows interface to send and receive your e-mails in Outlook or check your appointments while you are out of the office, and synchronizes with your PC when you return.

Choosing your ISP

If you are starting out with a new PC, the software for Windows and your applications will be pre-installed, but you will need to set up your access to the Internet and establish your e-mail account.

Windows includes an ISP referral service to help you select a suitable provider in your area.

You will find a much longer list of suitable ISPs, if you visit the ISP Buyer's Guide Web site at www.thelist.com and search by area code, country code or service type.

1 Open the folder C:\Program Files\Online Services, and double-click the Refer me to more Internet Service Providers icon.

2 The referral service will download a list of Internet service providers in your area. Choose the service you want to use.

The available options may vary according to where you are located and which version of Windows you are using.

You are not restricted to the above services, but you will require the setup procedure from the ISP concerned if you want to connect to a different service. You may also need special software. You can usually get this on CD-ROM, if you don't have alternative access to the Internet.

If you will be connecting to the Internet through a local area network, you'll need information from your network administrator, such as the name of the proxy server and the port number.

Your administrator may also provide special settings to configure your browser for corporate networks.

Setting up your Internet service

Select the service you want to use, or insert the appropriate setup CD and you will be taken through the process for defining your account. For example, if you choose the Virgin.net service, you'll follow these steps:

Check that the ISP has a local phone number for your area, a lo-call number charged at local call rates, or best of all a free (1800/1888) number.

1 Specify your details and the Internet Connection Wizard will dial the ISP provider, passing on the information you've specified.

2 Confirm your details, and specify the user name you'd like. This is added to the ISP server name to create your e-mail address.

If the user name you enter is already in use, you'll be asked to provide an alternative. This process will be repeated until a unique user name is found.

3 Complete the registration process, accepting terms and conditions, and record your sign-on details.

The connection will be automatically added, and your browser will be updated to use the new ISP account.

To connect to your account:

4 Select Start, then Connect To, then click your ISP account. There will initially be just one entry, but you can have additional connections defined.

Making the Internet connection

Select Start, Connect To, and choose the connection you want. If you have several accounts defined, see page 84.

Note that Windows saves your password by default. If you are not the only user on the system, clear the box so that the password is requested each time you connect.

Click Cancel if you want to work off-line (e.g. to view Web pages that you have previously downloaded).

If you are part of a local area network, you will not have to dial up to use the Internet, but will be connected automatically through the LAN.

You'll see a page like this if you've installed Virgin.net and accepted their default home page as your starting point.

1 Select Start, Internet Explorer to open your browser, and it will initiate the default connection with the Internet.

2 Check the user name and type the password (if required), then click the Connect button. The modem dials the supplied telephone number to connect to the ISP security server.

3 The server checks your user name and password. When this is completed, it passes control to the browser which will display your Internet startup page.

The Internet startup page would have been defined during registration, and is normally a News page related to the ISP service you are using. However, you can change this to another Web page (see page 17) if you wish.

You don't have to belong to a site to display its pages, except for those pages restricted to members only.

Change Home page

You don't have to use the ISP's default home page. You could choose a page on another Web site, or a page that you've published to your own Web space, or even a file that is stored locally on your hard disk. To select a new home page, you must change the Internet options.

Follow these steps:

1 Select Tools from the Internet Explorer Menu bar, and click Internet Options.

2 Type in the URL Web page address, for example: http://www.microsoft.com/office/outlook/default.asp.

Click Use Blank to start the browser without fetching a page from the Internet. Click Use Current, and the Web page currently open in the browser becomes your new home page.

3 From this screen you can clear the Internet file storage.

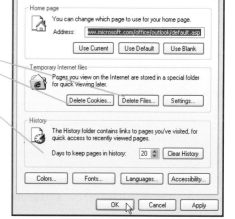

4 You can tell the browser how long to retain links to the pages that you've visited in the past.

5 When you've finished configuring your browser, click OK to save the new settings.

You may find it useful to specify a search engine Web site such as www.google.com as your home page.

6 The next time you start the browser, it will start up with the new home page. To display it immediately, without restarting, click the Home button on the standard toolbar.

Keeping track of your connection

1 Select Tools, Internet Options, then click the Connections tab.

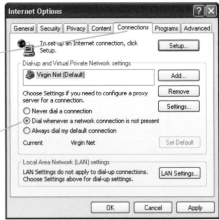

Internet Explorer will be set to dial whenever a network connection is not present.

When you terminate your Internet Explorer session, you'll be asked if you wish to disconnect from the ISP. This helps prevent staying connected when you've finished your tasks.

To provide a connection reminder:

2 Select Start, Connect To, Show all Connections. Right-click your ISP connection and select Properties.

3 Check Show icon in notification area when connected box, then click OK to save the change.

4 An icon will be added to the system tray whenever the connection is active. A message balloon will appear initially, showing the connection speed.

5 Right-click the icon at any time to display the Status or to immediately Disconnect.

The account details, including the e-mail address and your password, are added to Outlook Express during registration (see page 15).

Open Outlook Express and you'll find that the account details have been added, and an initial message from the ISP displayed. If you have another system available, or a helpful friend, get a message sent to that account to make sure you can receive mail there.

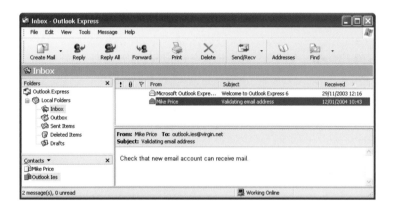

6 Select Tools, Accounts, select the new e-mail account, and then click the Properties button.

Click the Servers tab to see the definitions of incoming and outgoing servers. The sign-on details are also stored in this panel.

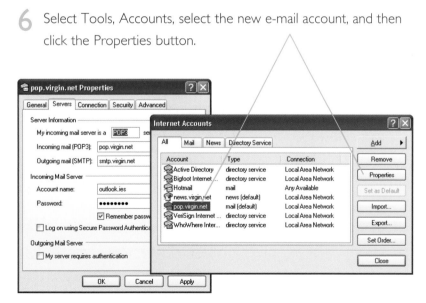

Installing Outlook

Outlook 2003 is provided as a part of Office 2003, so it will already be installed on your hard disk, if you have the Office suite installed.

To install Office 2003, if this is required:

1 Insert the Office CD-ROM, and the Setup program starts up automatically. Enter the CD key for your copy of Office.

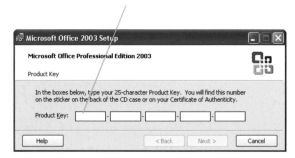

2 Type your name and company, confirm that you accept the terms and conditions, and then choose the type of installation.

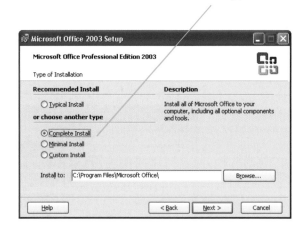

3 All the applications in your edition of Office 2003 will be installed. This will include Outlook 2003, whichever edition you have. See page 12 for details of the various editions.

Deleting the installation files saves about 272 MB disk space. However, if you can afford this space, leaving the files on the disk will be very useful in the future, when you need to repair or change your Office installation.

You do not have to supply any personal information when you activate and register (via Microsoft Passport), so that Microsoft can inform you directly when there are relevant changes or updates.

Activating your software associates it specifically with the particular hardware on which it is installed. You can install one copy of Office 2003 on two PCs – a desktop PC and a laptop PC, for example. If you change your hardware and want to transfer the software, you may need to contact Microsoft by telephone to activate the software on the new PC.

4 When the files have been copied and the applications configured, you are offered the opportunity to delete the installation files.

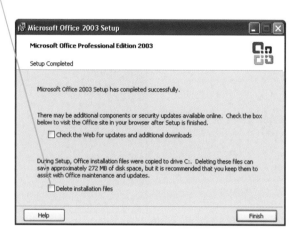

5 When you run any application, you are reminded to activate your software. Over the Internet is best, if your connection is set up.

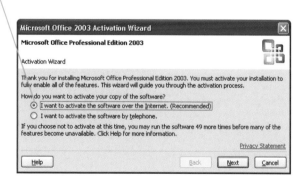

6 If you choose not to activate immediately, you can start Office 2003 up to 49 more times before it makes many features unavailable, until you do carry out activation.

Running Outlook for the first time

Outlook recognizes it is being started for the first time. The Startup wizard guides you through the steps in configuring Outlook 2003, configuring the accounts, importing messages and contacts, and creating the Welcome message.

Outlook will replace Outlook Express (or any other e-mail client installed on your PC). If you have already used your existing e-mail client, you will not lose your message logs, and you will not have to re-enter the names and e-mail addresses that you have accumulated. The installation procedure takes care of transferring these to your new system.

Outlook Express remains on your hard disk after Setup completes. It will be used by Outlook for accessing newsgroups, but you should no longer use it for e-mail.

1. Run Outlook from the E-mail entry in the Start menu, which has been updated from Outlook Express to Outlook 2003.

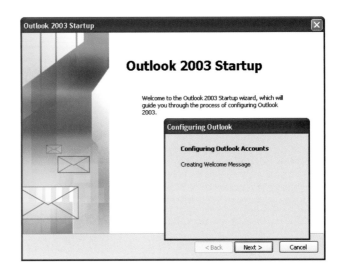

2. Choose the e-mail system from which you want to import e-mail messages, address books and settings.

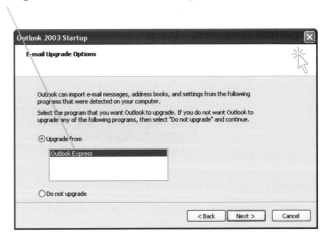

3. Confirm account details including Name, E-mail address, Server names, Account name and Password.

...cont'd

Setup allows you to add components that are available from the installation CD. Chapter 11 identifies other add-ins that can be downloaded from the Internet, from Microsoft or from other sources.

4 Startup will list the dialup connections defined on your system. Select the one defined by your ISP for your account.

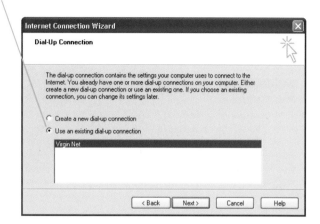

5 Click Yes to copy the e-mail messages and the name and address list from the old system to your new Outlook folders.

Only the main contact and mail details are migrated to Outlook 2003 when you upgrade from Outlook Express with Identities (configured with multiple user profiles).

6 When the wizard completes, Outlook starts with the accounts, contacts and messages defined.

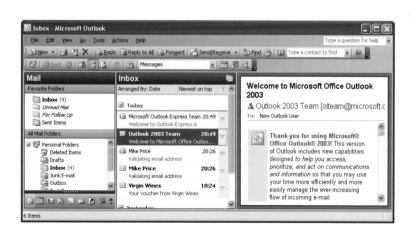

Starting Outlook

Outlook will be added to the Internet Options in Internet Explorer as the default E-mail Program.

1   Click the Mail button and select Read Mail to start Outlook with the Inbox displayed (or to switch to Outlook if already running).

2   Click New Message to switch to Outlook with a new mail message displayed ready for composing.

Outlook will quickly become an essential part of your system, and you may decide that you want it to start automatically every time you start the system. You can achieve this by adding Outlook to the Startup folder.

If you set Outlook to start up at power on, and you have a dial-up link, you should avoid setting auto dial for your e-mail accounts.

3   Left-click and drag the E-mail shortcut onto the Start menu. Hover over All Programs, then over Startup to open the folder.

The E-mail shortcut icon is copied when you drag and drop. However, if you drag and drop the Outlook 2003 shortcut from the Microsoft Office folder onto the Start menu, the shortcut is moved, not copied.

4   Drag the E-mail icon into the Startup folder, and release the mouse button to drop a copy of it there.

Each time you start the PC (or restart Windows), Outlook will automatically start up and display the Inbox or the Outlook Today view, depending on the startup option you've set (see pages 27-28).

Terminating Outlook 2003 is even easier:

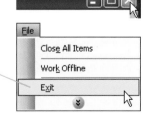

If you're not ready to Exit, but want to tidy up the session, select File, Close All Items to close all the open Outlook items (messages, tasks etc.) but leave Outlook active.

5   To end Outlook, click the Close button on the top right of the title bar, or select File, Exit from the menu bar.

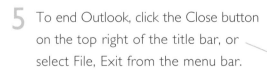

Exploring Outlook

In this chapter, you'll see the different interfaces that Outlook offers, control the way that Outlook starts up and runs, customize your Outlook environment, and switch between Outlook folders and functions using toolbars, navigation panes and shortcuts.

Covers

Chapter Two

The parts of Outlook

1 Start Outlook from the Startup folder, the Start menu or from Internet Explorer, to display the Inbox.

The default startup view shows the Inbox viewer, or you can select the Outlook Today overview (see page 27).

Menu bar   Navigation pane   Standard toolbar

Current folder   Advanced toolbar

Search help

The Outlook folders that you see depend on your installation and will differ if you are using Exchange Server for your e-mail.

The Outlook functions can be reached from the navigation buttons and icons, or from the Folder List (see page 31).

Buttons   Mail folders   Reading pane

Icons   Status bar   Current item

The exact look and content of the screens that you see will differ, depending how you have configured Outlook. For example, you can choose to reposition or to hide the Reading Pane.

2 Select View, Reading Pane and choose the setting: Right, Bottom or Off.

Starting with Outlook Today

Outlook Today gives a high-level view of the day's activities, highlighting the events and tasks that you will be facing. There are extracts from your calendar and your task list, plus a summary of your mail. You can change the amount and the type of information presented, for example to show the week ahead.

You can also display Outlook Today by clicking the Outlook Today button at the left end of the Advanced toolbar (see page 35).

The default start up with the Inbox is ideal if you want to go straight to work on your e-mail. If you use the full functions of Outlook however, you may prefer the alternative startup display, Outlook Today, which gives quick access to the main functions.

1 Click Personal Folders in the Mail Folders list, and select Customize Outlook Today.

2 Click the box to startup in Outlook Today.

3 Set the number of days in the calendar display.

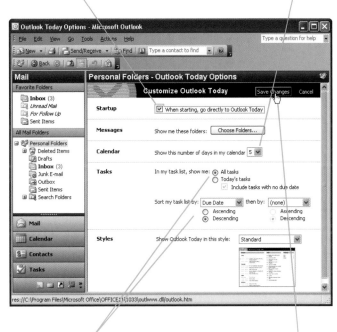

You can change the style of Outlook Today's window, to show the details in two columns or a single column.

You can change Outlook startup in other ways also. See page 28 for details of startup switches.

4 Choose All tasks or just Today's tasks and specify the sort options.

5 Press Save Changes (or Cancel) to return to Outlook Today.

The next time that you start Outlook, the Outlook Today window, with your selected settings for calendar and task lists, will be displayed first.

Controlling Outlook startup

To find details, search Help for "Control start up". You'll be referred to an entry in the Office Assistance Center on the Web (see page 38).

Outlook has a number of command line switches which allow you to start it in a specific mode or with a particular form or folder displayed.

Startup switches:

/folder	Hide the Navigation Pane
/select path/folder	Display the named folder
/c ipm.note	Create an e-mail message
/c ipm.activity	Create a journal entry
/c ipm.contact	Create a contact
/c ipm.stickynote	Create a note
/a "path:\filename"	New e-mail with the specified file attached
/profile profilename	Load the specified profile.
/nopreview	Hide Reading Pane, and remove option from the View menu.
/Safe	Without extensions, Reading Pane, or toolbar customization

You can also use the /c ipm switch to start up and create an appointment, contact, post, stickynote (i.e. a note) or task.

There are some additional switches that clear and regenerate certain types of item in Outlook:

You should note that paths or names which include spaces must be enclosed in quotation marks. For example: "C:\Program Files".

/cleanfreebusy	Clear free/busy information
/cleanreminders	Clear reminders
/cleanviews	Restore default views
/cleanschedplus	Clear Schedule+ data
/firstrun	Starts as for the first time.
/resetfolders	Restore missing folders
/resetnavpane	Rebuild the Navigation Pane

These could be very useful for resolving problems with the particular types of item, but they will delete information from the folders, so make sure to backup Outlook before trying these switches.
See Chapter 11 for information on Outlook backup and folder archives.

Using switches

Create a shortcut on the Desktop, to start Outlook with the required switches.

The easiest way to add switches is to create a shortcut on the desktop to the Outlook program:

Use Search to find the Outlook.exe file. Right-click the file icon and select Create Shortcut. Click Yes to create it on the desktop.

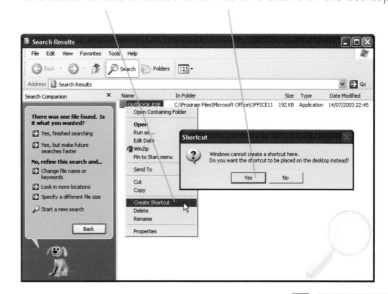

See page 146 to use switches to start up Outlook with a Note displayed.

To start Outlook with the Reading Pane switched off and with the Drafts folder displayed, add the switches:
/nopreview
/select outlook:drafts

2 Right-click the new shortcut icon and select Properties from the menu.

If you have set your folder options to use point to select, then you should single-click (rather than double-click) the Outlook shortcut.

3 Type the command line switches after the file name in the Target box, and click OK to save the changes.

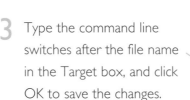

4 Double-click the shortcut on the desktop to startup Outlook with the specified switches applied.

Navigation Pane

The Outlook Bar featured in previous versions of Outlook has been replaced by the Navigation Pane, with a set of buttons and a button bar that select what contents are displayed in the pane.

1 Mail is the default pane, showing all the e-mail folders plus a set of Favorite folders.

You can also change the number of buttons displayed by selecting Configure Buttons and clicking Show More Buttons or Show Fewer Buttons.

2 If folders are hidden, scroll the list, or drag the separator bar to reveal more folders. Buttons that drop off are added as icons on the button bar at the foot of the pane.

3 Click the Calendar button or icon to show the Calendar Pane, which provides date navigation and also allows you to select a shared calendar (see page 109).

You could also click Add or Remove Buttons and select which buttons will be displayed in the Navigation Pane. The "tick" boxes in the list toggle buttons off and on.

4 Click Configure Buttons at the end of the button bar, and select Navigation Pane Options from the menu.

5 Choose in which order the buttons display, by selecting entries and clicking Move Up or Move Down. Clear the box alongside an entry to hide that button.

You may prefer to work from the Folders list, as you would have when using Outlook Express.

6 Click the Folder List button, or select Go, Folder List, or use the shortcut Ctrl+6 (there's a shortcut for each of the panes).

The Navigation Pane entry on the View menu is a toggle, and the pane is displayed when the entry is ticked. Alt+F1 will also toggle the display.

7 To allow extra space for the current folder, select View, Navigation Pane. Click again to redisplay, or simply select one of the panes from Go or by using a shortcut key.

You can also click and drag the vertical edge of the Navigation pane, to reduce its width and make more screen space available to the rest of the display items.

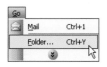

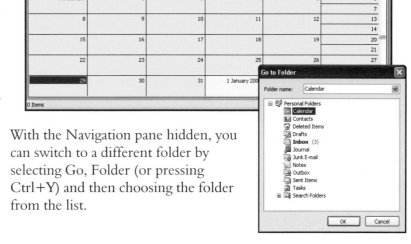

With the Navigation pane hidden, you can switch to a different folder by selecting Go, Folder (or pressing Ctrl+Y) and then choosing the folder from the list.

Shortcuts Pane

The Shortcuts Pane allows you to create shortcuts to Outlook folders, Office documents and other programs. As installed however, there are just two shortcuts defined.

See page 186 for details of using the Office Update Web site to update the Office applications, including Outlook.

HOT TIP

1 Click the Shortcuts button to display the Shortcuts Pane, with shortcuts to Outlook Today and to the Office (and Outlook) Update Web site.

Shortcuts

2 Click the Add New Shortcut button, and select an Outlook folder from the Folder name drop-down list, or from the folder tree, and click OK.

Right-click a shortcut to open it, open it in a new window, delete or rename it, or move it up or down in the list. You can also drag a shortcut up or down the list or drag it to another group.

DON'T FORGET

3 Click the Add New Group button and then type the name, to create a new group for shortcuts. It will be added at the bottom of the list.

4 By default, shortcuts are added to the first shortcut group. Right-click a group to add a shortcut to it, to rename it, to remove it, or to move it up or down in the list.

In previous versions of Outlook, you could select files and folders from the file system, but this facility has been withdrawn in Outlook 2003.

You can also add shortcuts for files, folders and programs to the shortcut groups, but you must use drag and drop for this.

5 Open the folder that contains the Windows file or folder you want to add to your Shortcuts.

6 Shrink the Outlook window so that you can view both the Shortcuts Pane and the Windows file you need at the same time.

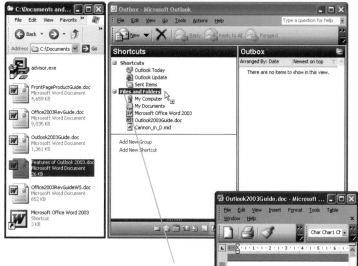

7 Drag and drop the Windows file or folder onto the title of the appropriate shortcut group.

You can right-click the shortcut to an Outlook folder or URL and select Open in New Window, and it displays another Outlook window with the requested item.

When you click on a shortcut to an Outlook folder or to a Web page, it opens in the information area within Outlook. When you click a document or data file, it opens the related program, in a separate window outside Outlook. File system folders open with Windows Explorer.

Menu bar and toolbars

Across the top of the Outlook window you'll find the Menu bar with File, Edit, View, etc. which display lists of commands and submenus. Below the Menu bar is the Standard toolbar, with buttons to give you quick access to the most used commands.

1 Switch to the Calendar and you'll see that the toolbar changes to suit. You'll also find new commands on the Menu bar.

2 Select View from the Menu bar and click Toolbars. Click the name of an un-ticked toolbar to display it. Click on a ticked toolbar to remove it.

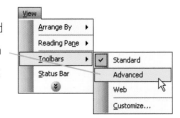

3 Click the move handle on a toolbar and drag it to a new location, e.g. put the Standard and the Advanced toolbar on same line.

You could also select Tools, Customize from the menu bar to display the Customize panel.

4 Select View, Toolbars, Customize from the menu bar, or right-click a toolbar and click Customize.

5 Click the Options tab to adjust the menu or toolbars. For example, choose to Show full menus, or select Large Icons for the toolbars.

Changes you make here will be immediately applied to all Office 2003 applications, not just Outlook 2003.

6 Click Close when you've made all the changes.

As you switch between the various folders in Outlook, the Advanced toolbar keeps track of the folders you've visited.

With the buttons on the Advanced toolbar, you can:

Try out the ways of moving around in Outlook, so you can decide which way helps you move quickly to wherever you want.

- Go to Outlook Today

- Go Back to the previous folder in the list

- Go Forward to the next folder in the list

- Move up one level in the folder list

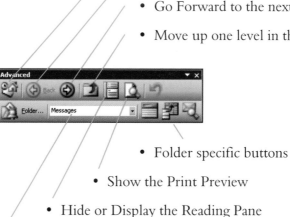

- Folder specific buttons

- Show the Print Preview

- Hide or Display the Reading Pane

- Change the current view

Customizing toolbars

You can add the Folders command as a button on one of the toolbars, to give you quick access to the folder list without having to make the Navigation Pane visible.

The Folder banner used to feature buttons that let you choose the Outlook folder you wanted to go to. These buttons don't appear in Outlook 2003, but you can add a button to one of the toolbars to give you this option.

1 Open the Customize panel (see page 35) and click the Commands tab.

You can create your own toolbar: select the Toolbar tab, click the New button, then add buttons to it using the Commands tab.

2 Select Go from the Categories box, and select Folder from Commands.

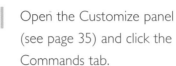

3 Drag the Folder command onto the Advanced toolbar, position the vertical marker after the Up One Level button, release the mouse button to insert the command, and Close Customize.

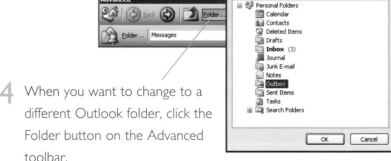

4 When you want to change to a different Outlook folder, click the Folder button on the Advanced toolbar.

Some change options are unavailable for buttons that display a list or a menu, and so appear grayed-out.

Change image and text for button

1 Switch to the function that uses the toolbar button you want to change.

2 Select Tools, Customize, drag the Customize panel out of the way, and right-click the button.

3 Modify the descriptive text name for the button, if this is required.

4 The name text can be shown on its own or with the image. The Default Style setting puts the image alone on the button.

5 Click Change Button Image, and choose one of the selection of images that Outlook offers, or use Copy/Paste from a bitmap image, or edit the image directly using a bitmap editor.

To cancel changes and return to the original settings, right-click the button and select Reset.

6 Select the Default Style setting for the button to show the image alone. The ScreenTip acts as a prompt.

7 Click the new image button to display the Go To Folder panel (as shown on page 36).

Getting help

As an example of using Help, we will search for information on the Outlook startup switches, discussed on pages 28-29.

The easiest way to find help in Outlook is using the Ask a Question Box on the Menu bar. It is usually shown by default, but if it is not already showing:

1   Right-click the Menu bar, select Customize, right-click the box that appears, click the Show Ask a Question Box, and then Close.

The Show Ask a Question Box option is a toggle, so repeating the process would hide the box from the Menu bar.

2   Type your search phrase, e.g. "startup switches", into the box and press Enter.

3   Note that there is a total of twenty results. Select the most suitable entry, in this case Command-line switches.

You will get additional and more up-to-date entries if you are connected to the Internet at the time you issue the search, since Outlook will automatically search Microsoft Office online.

4   The document from the Office Assistance Center is displayed. Click Auto Tile to view the Outlook and Help windows side by side.

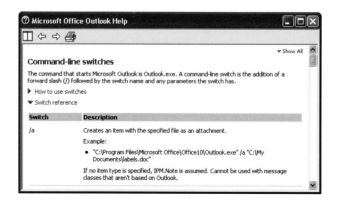

If the Task Pane is already visible, perhaps showing Search Results, click the Task Pane title bar and Help, to show the Outlook Help task pane.

5 Select Help from the menu bar and click Microsoft Office Outlook Help. This will display the Outlook Help task pane.

6 Click the Table of Contents link to display the list.

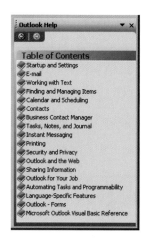

The Office Assistant is like the Ask a Question Box, but has a stylized display format and also has the habit of offering unsolicited advice from time-to-time.

7 If you are connected, it will download the latest copy, otherwise it displays the offline version. You can scroll through the chapters, enter a question, or search for particular terms in the Index.

Responding to popular demand, Microsoft has turned off the Office Assistant in Office 2003. However, this feature is still available if you find it useful or amusing.

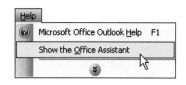

You can change the shape and the style of the Assistant, but the help offered stays much the same.

8 Select Help from the Menu bar and click Show the Office Assistant, then type your query and click Search. Select Help, Hide the Office Assistant if you decide it is no longer useful.

Help on the Web

Outlook 2003 and Office 2003 use Web pages on the Internet as a dynamic extension of the Help system.

If you don't find the information you need in the Help files, you can switch to the Internet to continue your search.

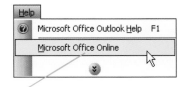

1 Click Help and choose Microsoft Office Online.

2 To search for help, click the Assistance link.

3 Search for general Office help, or scroll down and select the specific product.

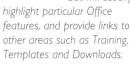

The contents of these Office Web pages will vary from time-to-time, but will usually highlight particular Office features, and provide links to other areas such as Training, Templates and Downloads.

4 This highlights topics of interest to Outlook users, and provides a search of Outlook 2003 assistance.

Using electronic mail

This chapter works through the basics of e-mail: sending a message, making copies, receiving messages, saving and printing messages, seeing how your messages make their way through the Internet, and replying to messages.

Covers

Chapter Three

Creating your message

Electronic mail (e-mail) is the computer equivalent of exchanging memos and notes. You can communicate with anyone who has access to the Internet, either directly through an ISP or through an office or college network. All you need is the e-mail address, in the form of a name and an address:

There's a variety of address formats and some are case sensitive, so type the e-mail address exactly as given to you, just to be sure, and avoid putting in any spaces.

userid@network

name/number (e.g. johns; jsmith; 76543.123, john.smith)

address of network (e.g. msn.com; aol.com; virgin.net)

required separator (say it as "at")

See page 27 in Chapter 2 to start Outlook in the Outlook Today window or with the Inbox folder displayed.

You can send and receive e-mail from any part of Outlook, but the normal starting point is the Inbox, which stores received messages. Start Outlook, and follow these steps to create a new message:

| If you started in Outlook Today, select Messages, or click Inbox on the Navigation Pane.

The Inbox will contain a list of messages right from the start. They are those transferred from your previous e-mail system during Outlook setup, plus some informational and marketing notes, sent to you as part of the install.

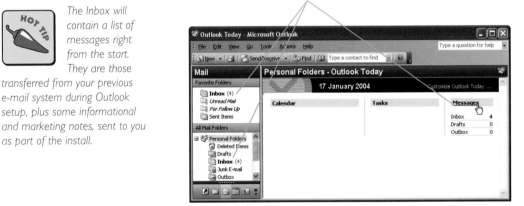

2 With the Inbox displayed, click New on the toolbar to start creating a message.

Contacts keeps track of e-mail addresses and adds the details for you. See Chapter 5.

You may not see all the message headers on your system, since some are optional. See page 45.

Netiquette conventions for e-mail and newsgroup messages differ between groups. If in doubt, be informal but polite.

You can use the Outlook Editor or Word to compose your messages, using RTF (rich text format) or HTML for a variety of text effects. If you are posting e-mail notes to a newsgroup, it's better to use plain text.

Click the Message Format button on the toolbar to change the message format.

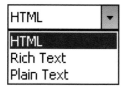

3 Type the e-mail address for the recipient, using the standard userid@network format, and add addresses for people getting Cc or Bcc copies (see page 45).

4 Type the Subject (the message title).

- Sender
- Recipient
- Copies
- Blind copies
- Subject
- Salutation
- Message text
- Sign off
- Signature text

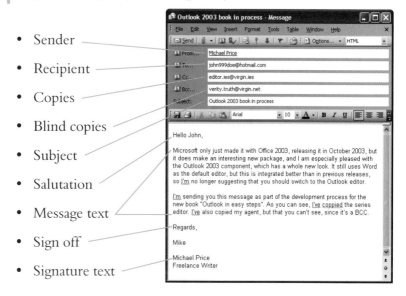

5 Issue a suitable salutation or greeting to the recipient, and introduce yourself if sending to someone new. This is considered good "Netiquette" – network etiquette.

6 Type the text of your message as the addressee should see it. The example shows Word with plain text. This is the best thing to do if you do not know what system is being used by the recipients. It also keeps the messages smaller.

7 End with your name and personal details, such as title or telephone number. You needn't put your e-mail address, since Outlook attaches this to the message when it is sent.

Checking spelling and grammar

While you are creating or changing your message, you can check the contents, using the full grammar and spelling check facilities from Word 2003.

1   Select Tools from the Menu bar and click Spelling and Grammar, or press the shortcut function key F7.

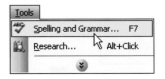

Each spelling error in the message is detected in turn, and you are usually offered one or more possible words. Potential grammar and style errors may also be indicated.

2   Locate the correct spelling (or retype the word) and Change the text. Click Change All to amend all occurrences in the note.

Press Options to change the settings, edit the supplement, or to switch off the grammar checking.

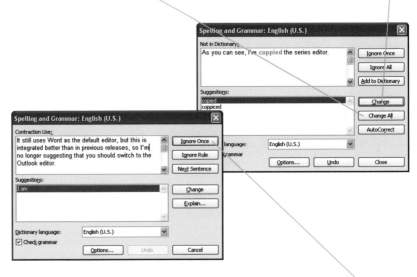

Outlook can check the spelling in other languages, e.g. Spanish or French, as well as English.

3   If the word detected is just a code or other value, press Ignore Once, or Ignore All if there may be more occurrences.

4   For proper names and for words not found, press Add To Dictionary to include them in the supplementary dictionary.

5   Spell check terminates when all the errors have been detected and processed (or when you click Cancel).

Message headers

Some of the boxes on the message header are normally hidden, but you can show them if you wish.

| Click the down-arrow on the Options button, to select the Bcc or the From headers.

Copy your own ID on messages where you need a particular record kept.

Bcc is for blind carbon copy (or courtesy copy) recipients. These receive a copy of the message but, unlike Cc (carbon copy) recipients, their details are not listed on the message. This is a useful technique when you want to send copies of messages to a log kept for record keeping or personal use.

Click the priority buttons on the toolbar, to draw attention to the relative importance of a message. There's a high importance and a low importance button.

2 Click to select or deselect. The two buttons in combination are used to represent Normal, High, and Low priorities.

3 Click the Flag button to set a reminder to take action later. You can set a date and time, and a purpose.

The flag and the priority fields can be used to identify or sort the entries in the message folders.

Saving messages

 Outlook automatically saves open messages every three minutes, storing them in the Drafts folder. They are removed when the message is sent, or when you Close and discard.

1 With an open message, select File from the Menu bar, and click Close to stop editing.

2 Click Yes to save and end, No to discard and end, or Cancel to return to message edit.

3 Select Tools from the Menu bar, then Options, click the Preferences tab and click the E-mail Options button.

 You can turn automatic saving off or on, and change the time, or the target folder for saving unsent messages. You can also set the options for saving sent messages.

4 Select or clear the Automatically save unsent messages box.

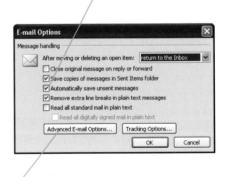

If auto save has been turned off, or if you want to be sure that the message is saved, carry out a manual save by clicking the Diskette button.

5 Press Advanced E-mail Options to change the target folder and the frequency for saving.

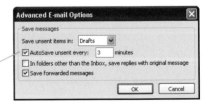

Sending messages

Messages

Inbox	4
Drafts	1
Outbox	0

1 If you have saved your message in the Drafts folder, select My Shortcuts, Drafts and double-click the message to re-open it.

2 Outlook reminds you that this message has not been sent. Type the rest of the message, and check that it is ready to go.

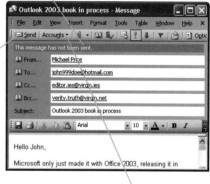

3 Click the Send button to use the default (or only) e-mail account.

4 If you have more than one e-mail account (see page 84), click the Accounts button and choose the account you wish to use, then click Send.

5 Check in the Folders List or in Outlook Today that the Outbox count has increased. Open the Outbox folder to see the titles of the messages that are waiting to be transmitted.

Messages

Inbox	4
Drafts	0
Outbox	1

If your PC is connected to a local area network with a mail server such as Microsoft Exchange, messages will be immediately transferred to the server. You can recall or replace the message as long as the recipient is logged on using Outlook, and has not yet read the mail from the Inbox.

With Internet mail, Send really means "make ready to send", and the message waits as a pending item in the Outbox, until the next time Outlook checks for mail, or until you click Send/Receive.

Transmitting your message

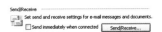
If you close Outlook without connecting to the Internet and explicitly or implicitly requesting transfer, it reminds you that there is mail waiting to go.

1 Click No to carry on and connect now, or click Yes and complete the process when you restart.

2 When you restart, the Outbox in the Folder List or Outlook Today shows the count of unsent mail. Press Send/ Receive to begin transmission.

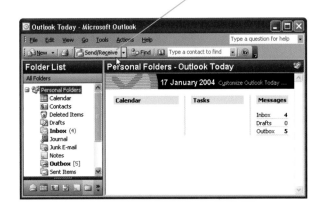

The Sign-in program dials your ISP, verifies your user ID and password and connects you to the mail server.

The messages from your Outbox are copied over the modem to the mail server, from where they will eventually be transferred to the recipients.

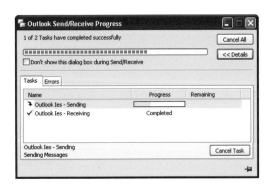

If you don't want to keep copies of sent mail, make sure that the "Save copies of messages in Sent Items folder" box in the E-mail Options panel is clear (see page 46).

The messages are removed from the Outbox to show that they have now been sent. Copies may be saved in the Sent Items folder in My Shortcuts. Outlook will normally disconnect from the Internet, and the mail server will handle the rest of the transfer.

3   Look in the Folder List or Outlook Today, to check that the sent messages have been moved from the Outbox, and look in the Sent Items folder to see copies of what was sent.

Sent messages are stored as "Read" so you don't get a count on the Sent Items folder icon. However, you can still open the messages to view the contents.

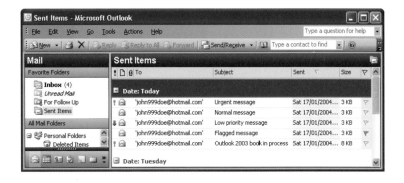

You can send mail without collecting any waiting messages, if you don't want to risk a large download. In this case, instead of Send/Receive, you use the Tools menu:

Outlook empties the Outbox folder, transfers messages to the Sent Items folder and the mail server, and then disconnects from the Internet without waiting for incoming mail. You will download this mail as usual the next time you press Send/Receive and connect to the mail server.

4   Select Tools from the Menu bar, choose Send/Receive, Send All and sign-on to your ISP account as usual.

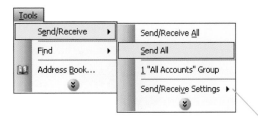

5   Click Send/Receive Settings for options to define Send/Receive groups, or to disable/enable Scheduled Send/Receive.

Routing messages over the Internet

Sender

Examine the route messages take over the Internet, to see where delays and errors could arise.

If you've set your mail to send automatically, you don't have to press Send/ Receive to initiate the process.

When messages have multiple recipients, only one message is sent to the server. The server generates the copies, including a Cc or Bcc back to the originator, if indicated.

You should note that transmission delays can occur at various points in the flow, including:

- *waiting to connect (step 3)*
- *over the Internet (step 9)*
- *waiting to connect (step 11)*
- *waiting to read (step 16)*
- *waiting to reply (step 18)*

1 Create the message (in-process copy saved in the Drafts folder).

2 Press Send to transfer the message to the Outbox folder.

3 Press the Send/Receive button to begin the transmission.

4 Encode the message and the attached items for transmission.

5 Dial the Sender's ISP mail server, and provide sign-on details.

6 Transmit the message to the Mail Server for interim storage.

7 Transfer the message to the Sent Items folder as a record.

8 Disconnect Sender from the Mail Server and transfer the message to the Sent Items folder.

9 Forward the message to the network address (or issue Failure Notice to Sender if the supplied address was invalid).

...cont'd

Problems may arise during encode and decode on systems with different capabilities.

10 Store message at the ISP in recipient's mail box (or issue Failure Notice if invalid ID).

11 Recipient presses the Send/ Receive button to get mail.

12 Dial the Recipient's ISP and provide the sign-on details.

With "always on" connections such as DSL and Cable, the dial step isn't required.

13 Transmit the message from the ISP mail server.

14 Decode message to standard text and attachments

Messages may be forwarded by many Internet servers before they reach their final destination.

15 Filter and store message in the Inbox or other folder selected by Rules Wizard.

16 Recipient opens and reads the message and views attachments.

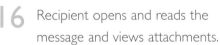

As well as the normal typed response, replies may include an automatic receipt or reading acknowledgment.

17 Create a reply to the message, (e.g. automatic confirmations).

18 Repeat the whole process in the reverse direction, to give the reply to the original Sender.

Recipient

Receiving messages

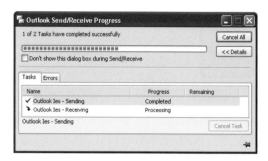

1   Press Send/Receive to download waiting messages:

2   Select Inbox from the Mail pane and note that messages are listed in a two-line format, with new unread messages shown in bold font.

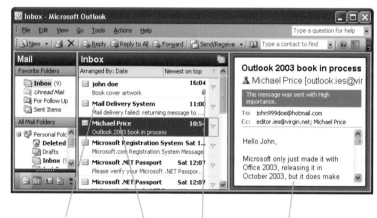

- Failed delivery.

- Cc sent back to originator.

- Message with file attachment.

- Selected message displayed in the Reading Pane.

3   Turn off the Reading Pane to get a one-line format for the list.

Reading the message

You don't always have to open the message. You can deal with e-mail straight from the folders. The subject and the Preview Pane mean that there's often no need to open a message. Outlook can check and process many items for you, using the Rules Wizard to filter your mail (see page 96).

If a specific button doesn't show on your toolbar, click the Toolbar Options button to see the overflow buttons, then click the Add and Remove Buttons to check which buttons have been hidden.

You don't have to return to the Inbox to read the rest of your messages, you can just request the next message.

Since you can sort messages into any order (see page 88), "previous" and "next" refer to the sequence of messages as displayed in the folder, not the date sent or received.

When you identify a message that needs action, open it to see the full contents in a separate window, and to get a toolbar for the actions you might take.

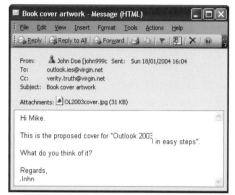

1 In the Inbox, double-click the message title.

2 Read the message and decide what action you need to take, using the toolbar buttons to help.

Reply Forward Print Flag Map Scroll messages Font Size

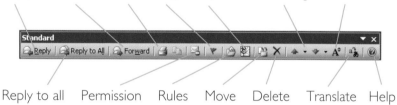

Reply to all Permission Rules Move Delete Translate Help

The toolbar shows the main actions at your disposal. There are various ways of replying (see page 54), you can move, delete or flag a message (see page 45), and you can change the display font size.

3 Click the Up button to move to the previous message in the list, or Down for next message.

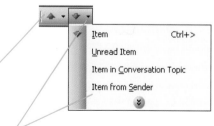

4 Click the expansion arrow to move Up or Down by category – Unread Item, Item in Conversation Topic, Item from (same) Sender, etc.

Replying to one or all

1 Click the Reply button to open a message form in a new window.

2 The sender's e-mail address is inserted, the subject title is added and RE: is entered as the prefix.

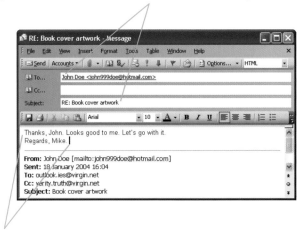

3 Insert your reply text, or make comment on the text of the original message, then press Send to put the reply in the Outbox.

As an alternative, you can tell Outlook to put prefixes in the original text, or send the original text as an attachment.

4 Select Tools, Options, click the Preferences tab, and click the E-mail Options button.

5 Click the arrows to pick an action, then click OK to apply the changes.

...cont'd

Replies to all will be sent to every address in the To box and the Cc box (though not the Bcc box), so check there are no inappropriate names, or unexpected omissions.

6 Click Reply to All, check the list of names, add the response, and press Send.

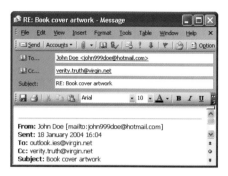

7 If you just want to send a message to a new name, click Forward on the original message and type the recipient's e-mail address.

The bitmap icons in the Inbox message lists tell you what action was last carried out with the message:

     Read

     Replied to

     Unread

     Forwarded

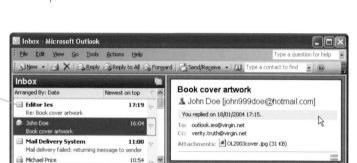

8 When you've sent the reply or forwarded the message, the bitmap on the Inbox message list changes. When you view the message, there's also an Info note to say you've replied.

9 Click the Info note to run an advanced search that looks in all the message folders and all the related messages, replies and forwards:

The search facilities can be used to collect together all the Outlook items related to a topic, not just messages.

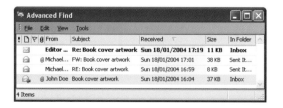

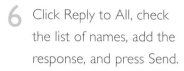

Adding your signature

Outlook lets you specify two signatures, for new mail and replies. You can have additional signature files to suit various situations, and insert the one that is appropriate to a given message.

Outlook allows you to specify a block of text to attach as a signature for the messages you send. To define the text for your signature:

1 Click Tools, Options and select the Mail Format tab.

2 Choose entries from the lists or click Signatures to edit or create new ones.

You might like to add a comment or thought for the day, as part of the signature.

3 Type the text you want for your signature file. With RTF or HTML selected, you can choose fonts and text effects.

If you've defined an electronic business card (vCard), you can add it to your signature. (See page 78 for details of vCards).

4 Click OK to save the text, and the next time you create a message the signature will appear, formatted or in plain text.

Remember that your recipients may, for some reason, have to view your messages in plain text, where all the fonts and text effects are removed. To see what they will get, select Message Format, Plain Text.

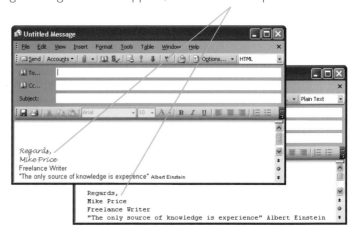

Attaching files

There is no Insert, Item with Word as the editor. Instead, click the arrow next to the paperclip symbol on the toolbar and select Item:

Click Yes if you want the file sent. See page 183 to receive this type of file.

When you send an e-mail message you can attach images, documents, spreadsheets, etc. The file names appear as icons in the message header. When the message arrives, the recipient can save the files to disk, or open them directly from the message. This assumes that the software needed to process the particular file type is installed on the recipient's system.

1 With the message open, and the cursor positioned in the text, choose Insert from the Menu bar and then select File.

2 You can look in folders on your hard disk or on networked drives. Select all of the file names you want, and then click Insert.

3 Click the down arrow, and select Insert as Text, to add the contents to the body of the message.

4 Icon placeholders will be added to the message header.

5 A copy of each file will be sent along with the message, when you press the Send button.

Inserting pictures

Messages that use HTML format can have pictures, lines and hypertext links inserted directly into the body of the message, in the most appropriate position and viewable immediately. To include a picture in the message:

1 Open the message in HTML format. Position the cursor in the text. Select Insert, Picture, From File.

2 Look in your local or networked data folder (see page 57) to find the image you wish to include. Select the file (normally type .jpg or .gif) and click Insert.

3 Click the picture to display the Picture toolbar and select Picture Format, to position the picture relative to the text:

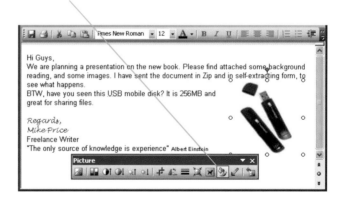

4 From Picture Format, you can also apply borders, or select the Web tab, and specify alternative text to display while loading.

Fancy stationery

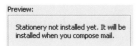
1 Select Actions from the Menu bar, and then New Mail Message Using.

2 Choose a stationery type from the quick list, or request More Stationery to see the list of available types.

3 Select the types in the Stationery panel to see their effect. Choose the one you want and click OK to open the new message form.

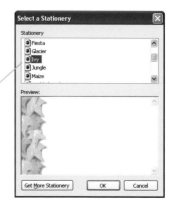

4 If this is the first time you have used that type, it will be installed into Outlook.

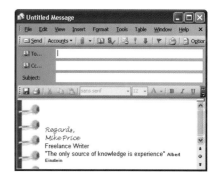

5 If you want an e-mail stationery type as the default for all of your messages, select Tools, Options from the main window and click the Mail Format tab.

6 Click the Stationery Picker button, select the stationery type as above, then click OK to save the new setting.

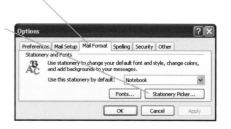

Receiving attachments

- *Prohibited types are blocked.*
- *Permitted types are seen as icons.*
- *Inserted pictures will be shown as icons and are also displayed, if you have the required viewer. Otherwise, you will see the descriptive text instead.*

Outlook 2003 prompts you for Level 2 files such as .xls or .doc. It will completely block Level 1 files such as .bas (Visual Basic) and .sct (script) files. This is a precaution to protect your system from damage. See page 183 for further details.

The copy of the file remains in the Outlook folder even when you Save it to disk. You can select Remove from the attachment menu to eliminate the copy of the file and free-up the disk space.

1 Open the message with attachments. Note the message in the Infobar which tells you that the .exe file has been blocked.

2 Right-click an attachment icon to see the options to Open, Print, Save As, Remove or Copy the file.

3 Select Open, or double-click an icon and the attachment will be opened. You'll be warned if the file is an executable type and hence could contain viruses.

4 You don't have to open the message to get permitted files. Select the Inbox entry, click File, Save Attachments and you see a list of the files.

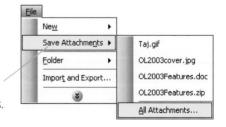

Managing contacts

This chapter looks at keeping track of contact details, starting with e-mail addresses for messages, and adding in all the other details about the people you meet and deal with.

Covers

Chapter Four

Contacts and address books

If you are running Outlook 2003 on a stand-alone PC, or on a peer-to-peer network, without access to Exchange server or Windows server, the Contacts folder should be the only address book you have to worry about. You will have the Windows Address Book installed, but you should simply avoid using it.

Contacts folder

The Contacts folder in Outlook 2003 is your e-mail address book and information storage for the people and businesses you want to communicate with. In it you store e-mail addresses, mail addresses, phone numbers, pictures, birthdays, anniversaries, and any other information you may have concerning that contact. Outlook organizes the information that you enter, and lets you sort it by various characteristics, to make it easier to find a contact. Once you've located the contact entry, you can select a menu command or click a button to issue a meeting request, or assign a task to the contact, or

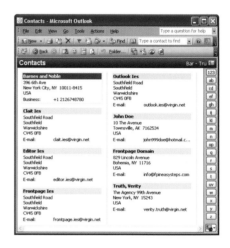

If you are a part of a small organization or business, you can store even more information about your contacts, including attachments, pictures, business notes, and product information, using the Business Contact Manager, the add-in designed for business contacts and sales opportunities. See pages 164-174 for more details.

dial the contact's phone number. The information can also be used for mailing labels, mail merge letters, Publisher documents, or any application that requires information about people or businesses. In most cases, this will be the only contacts list you need worry about.

Address Book

As well as the Contacts folder, Outlook 2003 has an Address Book. This is actually a collection of address books or address lists, which you use to look up and select names, e-mail addresses, and distribution lists for messages. When you start typing a name in the To, Cc, or Bcc box, Outlook automatically checks to see if there's a match in the Address Book, and if so supplies the rest of the address, or you can select a name from the list. The Address Book is also used for Find a contact function on the Standard toolbar. The types of address books that can be displayed in the Outlook Address Book include:

You need only be concerned with the global address book if you are part of an organization and need to share address book information with others in the group.

Global Address List

When you are using an Exchange Server e-mail account, the Global Address List contains the names and e-mail addresses of everyone in your organization. It can also contain global distribution lists and public folder e-mail addresses. This address list is managed by your system administrator.

Outlook Address Book

The Outlook Address Book is created automatically and contains those contacts in your Contacts folder that have e-mail or Fax entries. If you create additional contact folders, you can set the properties on each folder to include the contacts as part of the Outlook Address Book.

Internet directory services (LDAP)

Internet directory services are used to find e-mail addresses that are not in your local address book or the global address list.

Windows Address Book can be opened in Outlook Express, or from the Windows XP Start menu. Select Start, All Programs, Accessories, Address Book.

Personal Address Book

This is an older type of address list that can no longer be created using Outlook. If you do have information in a personal address book, you are recommended to import the contents into the Outlook Contacts folder.

Other address books

Some applications may have their own dedicated address books, and these may be added to Outlook as Additional Address Books.

Windows Address Book

The Windows Address Book stores e-mail addresses, mailing addresses, phone and fax numbers and is used by Windows programs, including Outlook Express, but it isn't included as part of the Outlook Address Book. The contacts that it contained would have been migrated to the Outlook Contacts folder when Outlook 2003 was installed, or you can import contacts from the Windows Address Book at any time.

Contacts folder

Select Go, Contacts, or press Ctrl+3, or click the Contacts button in the Navigation Pane to open the Contacts folder.

Initially the only entries present will be the contacts imported from Outlook Express (or other existing e-mail system) when Outlook 2003 was installed.

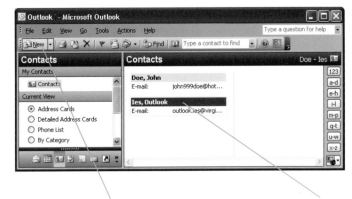

2 Press the New Contacts button to create a new entry, or double click an existing entry to open it and view or change the details.

The default view is for business information, but you can specify home or other details as well (or instead).

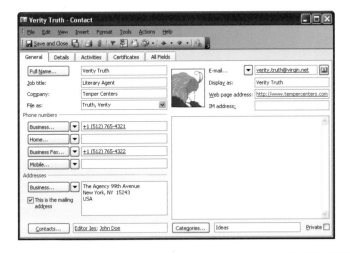

Outlook takes the full name and separates it into Title, First, Middle, Last and Suffix. If you enter a partial name, it decides which parts belong where.

3 Type the full name, and click the Full Name button to see how Outlook has interpreted the name. Select the Title or Suffix from the lists provided.

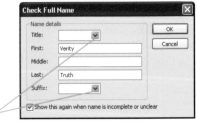

...cont'd

The File As field is used in the normal view to sort the names and addresses, in last-name order, but you can override this (see page 70).

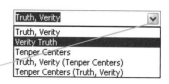

4 Outlook creates the File As entry based on the full name. Click the down-arrow for other suggestions.

5 Click on the large button, and select an image file to associate with the contact record, typically a passport-style photograph.

6 Type the e-mail address, and check the display name. Click the arrow to get spaces for any additional e-mail addresses.

The default view is for business information, but you can specify home or other details as well (or instead).

7 Provide a Web page URL and an Instant Messaging ID if these are available for this contact.

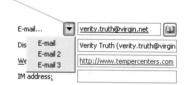

8 Select the Address type and type the full address details, then click the Address button to check how Outlook has interpreted the parts of the address.

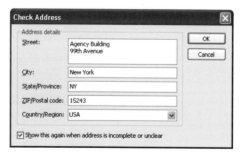

Outlook predefines 20 general categories that you can use to classify contacts and other Outlook items. You can add your own categories as required. See page 72 for more information.

9 Other items of data you could enter include related Contacts, associated Categories and a Private indicator for personal contacts. Click Save and Close to finish the record.

💾 Save and Close

Adding more contacts

You can use an existing contact as a model to create another contact, so you only need to add the changed information.

The Contacts folder is not just for people. As this example shows, you can use it to store information about projects, or about resources such as meeting rooms or projection equipment.

1 Open the original contact, check its details, then click Actions, New Contact from Same Company.

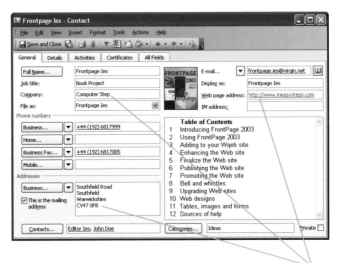

2 Company name, business phone, business address and Web page address are replicated, and you can add the remaining data.

3 Select an existing contact, and select Edit, Copy and Edit, Paste, to create a duplicate.

If the new contact details are mostly the same as an existing contact, duplicate it and then make the necessary changes.

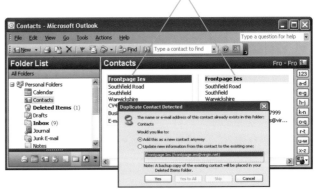

4 Edit the duplicate, changing the name, etc. then click Save and Close.

Sender and recipient fields on incoming messages can be used to update your Contact list in Outlook. To extract the e-mail details:

5 Open the message from the Inbox (or view it in the Reading Pane), then right-click one of the e-mail addresses.

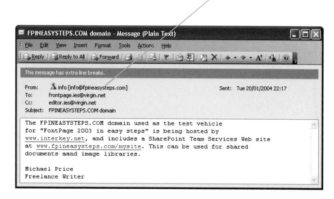

Unlike Outlook Express and previous editions of the full product, Outlook 2003 does not allow you to automatically add e-mail addresses when you reply to messages from new contacts.

6 Select Add to Outlook Contacts to create an entry. Add other details such as phone numbers. Then click Save and End.

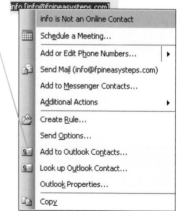

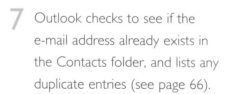

Select Add to Outlook Contacts to add this as a new contact anyway, even if you have several entries that share the same e-mail address.

7 Outlook checks to see if the e-mail address already exists in the Contacts folder, and lists any duplicate entries (see page 66).

8 If the e-mail entry already exists, you can select Look Up Outlook Contact to check other details.

9 Repeat this process for any other new e-mails in the message.

Importing contacts

You may have existing name and address data in another Windows application, in a database, or in a file downloaded from the Internet. Bring the contents into your Outlook Address Book, using the file import facility.

You can also import contact details from a vCard, which is an electronic business card (see page 78).

The first time you choose a particular data format, you may be asked to install the translator. If you saved your installation files to disk (see page 21) Outlook won't require the installation CD.

1. Select File from the Menu bar and choose Import and Export.

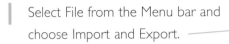

2. Select Import Internet Mail and Addresses to add contacts from Outlook Express or Eudora address books.

3. For other sources, select Import from another program or file.

4. Choose a supported application, or use Comma Separated Values, in Windows or DOS format for other sources of data.

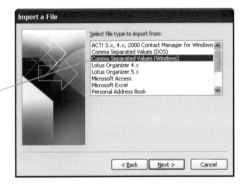

Most applications allow you to extract data fields with commas between them, one line per record, forming a comma-delimited file which Outlook can interpret.

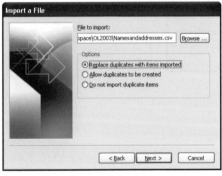

5. Select the data file from the hard disk, and then specify what to do with any duplicate records that may be detected.

6 Choose the Outlook folder to store the new contacts, either the Contacts folder or in this case, a subfolder of it. Click Map Custom Fields to see how Outlook has interpreted the data.

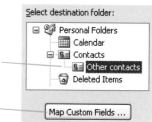

If you choose the same field names as Outlook uses for contacts data, the mapping will be automatic. If the names are different, drag field names from the source file to the appropriate destination field.

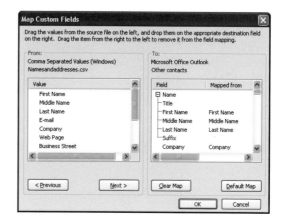

7 Click OK and then Finish. Outlook imports the data from the source file to the Other contacts subfolder.

New name and address details are stored in the Address Book, and duplicate names are detected and processed as requested. Open any invalid or incomplete entries, and change or add details.

Select any invalid or incomplete entries, and click Properties to correct any errors and to add any additional contact details that you may have available, to the appropriate destination field.

8 To make these contacts available as e-mail Address Book entries, right-click the subfolder, and select Properties. Click the Outlook Address Book tab and make sure that the folder is checked.

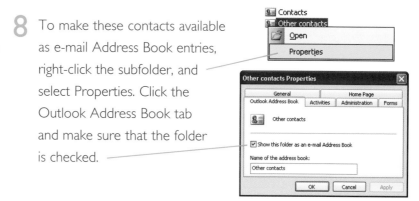

Viewing Contacts

1 The default view for Contacts shows Address Cards. To see other views available, select View, Arrange By, Current View.

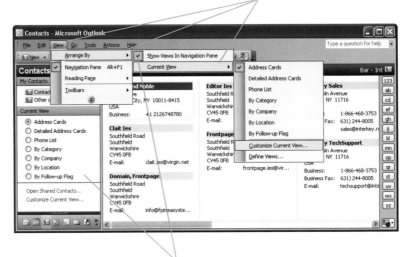

The first two views are in Card format, while the remaining views use the List format (see page 71 for an example of list view).

2 If the View option to Show Views in Navigation Pane is selected, you can also select views from there.

3 Select Customize Current View to make changes to the presentation.

You can select any address book field for sorting, even if the field is not actually displayed in the view. You can also limit the number of entries displayed using filter values. See page 72 for other ways to view your contact list.

You can, for example, click the Sort button and change the sort fields to use Company as the primary sort field, and Last Name as the secondary sort field.

4 Click the Reset Current View button to undo all changes and return to the original settings.

Phone directory

The Contacts folder Phone List view acts as a phone directory, showing all your contacts with their business, fax, home and mobile numbers, or whatever fields you decide you'd like to see in this view of contacts.

Select Phone List from the view list in the Navigation Pane, to see the contacts in a list format with telephone numbers.

When you enter phone numbers for contacts, provide the area or city code and the local number, and if you have contacts in other countries, make sure that you always specify the country or region, and Outlook will format the number. For example, you might enter:
  1234567890
Outlook would format this as:
  +1 (123) 4567890   (US)
  +44 (123) 45677890   (UK)
  +51 (123) 45677890   (Peru)
according to the country entered.

Select Customize Current View and click the Fields button to choose the types of phone numbers to display.

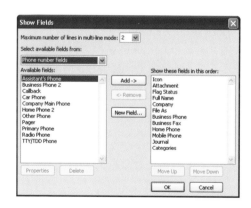

Press Add or Remove to revise the selection of phone number fields. Select an entry and click Move Up or Move Down to re-sequence the fields.

Choose Phone number fields from the Select available fields from option. Then choose the fields you want from the Available fields list, put them into the desired order, and click OK.

Organizing by category

Outlook items can be assigned several categories. You can define them when you create the records, or add them later.

You can assign other Outlook items such as messages and tasks to the same categories as the associated contacts. This will allow you to search for items of all types that belong together, and view or print them as a group.

Select the first contact, hold down the Shift key and click the last contact in the list. Hold down the Ctrl key to add additional contacts.

The same contact may appear in a number of different categories.

1 Open Contacts in a list view such as Phone List, select Tools, Organize, and then select Using Categories.

2 Specify a new category such as In Easy Steps and click Create to add it to the list.

3 Select a category from the list, then select all the contacts that are associated with that category.

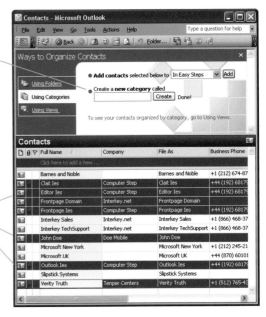

4 Click Add and the Categories field will be updated for each contact.

5 Close Organize and switch to Contacts, Category View. Click the [-] button to contract a list, and click the [+] button to expand a list.

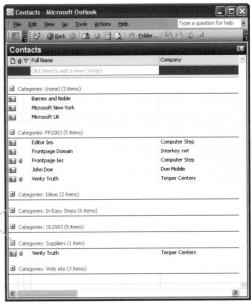

In any of the views, you can use Categories and other values to display only a specific subset of contacts, using the Filter option.

6 Open Contacts in any view, for example Address Cards, select Customize Current View from the Navigation Pane, and click the Filter button.

7 Type a Category value (or values) and click OK.

You'd click the Contacts tab to specify values for the address fields or Company, and click More Choices to specify attributes including Categories.

8 The Filter button is updated to show that a selection has been set. Click OK to apply the filter to the view.

Only contacts that have been assigned the specified category (or categories) will be shown.

The note in the Status bar reminds you that a Filter has been applied. However, the count continues to apply to the total number of items (not just the filtered results).

9 Select Customize Current View and click Reset Current View to remove the filter and display all the contacts again.

Addressing e-mails

The Outlook Address Book, based on the Contacts folder, makes it much easier and more accurate to send e-mail. Just choose entries from the list when you create a new message.

1 Click the New Mail Message from the Inbox, or press Ctrl+N to display the Message form.

2 Click any Select button (To:, Cc: or Bcc: if displayed) to specify recipients.

3 Choose name(s) from the list and click the To:, Cc: or Bcc: buttons to add the selection to the box.

If you have a lot of entries in the book, type the first few letters of the name, and Outlook will reposition the list.

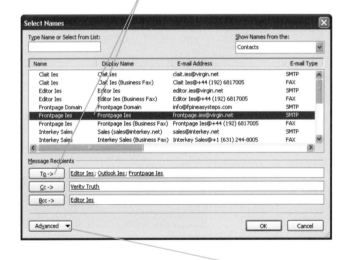

Note that there are multiple entries for those contacts that have fax phone numbers, or more than one e-mail address defined. Note also that, if you specify a contact for Bcc:, the header will be added to the message, even if it was not originally displayed.

4 To add a contact that isn't already in the Contacts folder, click the Advanced button and select New.

If you want to change your mind about a recipient, just right-click the contact entry display name and select Cut.

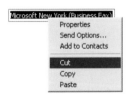

5 Select New Contact, choose In the Contacts (or In this message only) and click OK to define the contact details.

6 When you finish specifying the recipients, click OK to return to the Message form. The contacts are inserted in the header fields.

The names are underlined to show that they represent e-mail addresses. Right-click and select Properties to see the details. When you type in display names directly, the lookup takes place when the message is saved or sent, so you won't immediately see proper capitalization and underlining.

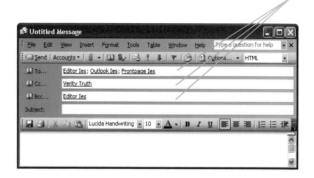

Check names

You can ask Outlook to check the name that you are typing, without opening the address book.

When you type a name you've used before, Outlook suggests possible matches, refining its guess as you type. Click a suggestion to select it.

Type the first part of the name, then click the Check Names button (or press Ctrl+K). Outlook lists the matching entries, so you can select the right one.

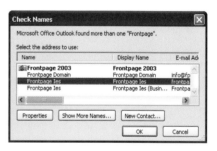

Outlook lists the matches it knows, getting progressively closer until there's only one match. However, you can click an answer at any point to complete the entry.

Creating distribution lists

When you have a large Contacts list and send lots of e-mail messages, you may find it helpful to create groups of contacts and use these to address your e-mails.

Click Add New to enter details for contacts not currently in the Contacts folder. Click the Add to Contacts box, and the details you provide are added to the Contacts folder as well as the distribution group.

If you have subfolders in your Contacts folder, you can select contacts from those also.

You can assign categories to distribution lists, just as you do for Contacts and other Outlook items.

1 Select File, New, Distribution List (or press Ctrl+Shift+L).

2 Type the name for the group, and click Select Members to add contacts.

3 Select one or more names and click Members to add them to the list.

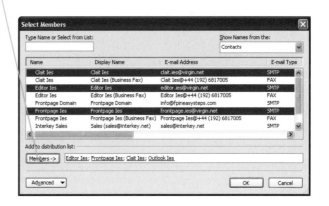

4 When you've added all the contacts for the list, click OK, check the result, then click Save and Close.

The named distribution list is added to your Contacts folder.

Distribution lists are shown in bold text in the Contacts folder, to distinguish them from ordinary entries.

5 Double-click the group name to list the entries in the group, and add or remove members.

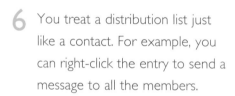

Note that the same name may appear in several groups. Changes to details for the name will be applied to all the groups it belongs to. When you delete a name from the Address Book, it will also be removed from any groups that it belonged to.

6 You treat a distribution list just like a contact. For example, you can right-click the entry to send a message to all the members.

7 You can add other contacts, using distribution lists and single contact entries. The list names are shown in bold text.

When you send the message and it arrives at the recipient's PCs, the actual contact display names are shown in the message headers, rather than the distribution list names.

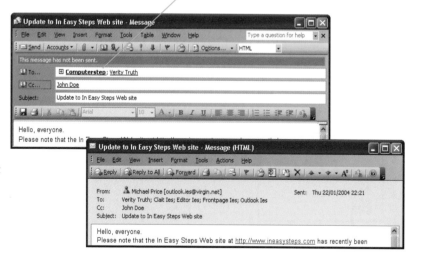

Using electronic business cards

Outlook supports the vCard standard for exchanging personal data. This is an electronic business card attached to the e-mail messages you send or receive. It can be used to update address books and contact lists.

Before creating your vCard, check your own entry in your address book to make sure the entries are complete and appropriate for the purpose.

When you create a signature (see page 56) Outlook provides three versions - .htm, .rtf and .txt - to use for HTML, Rich Text Format and Plain Text messages, respectively.

1 Select Tools, Options, and click the Mail Format tab. Click Signatures to display your list of signatures.

2 Choose the signature that is to have a vCard attached, and click Edit.

3 Since there's no vCard defined for this e-mail account, click New vCard from Contact.

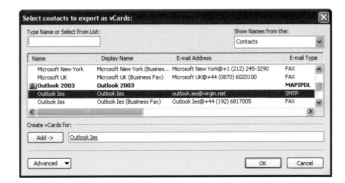

4 Locate the appropriate entry in the Contacts List, and click the Add button. You can create vCards for yourself or for others. Click OK to complete.

5 With the vCard defined, you can now select it from the list to apply to your messages.

This process creates a .vcf plain text vCard file in the same folder as your signature files. These are typically stored in: C:\Documents and Settings\User\Application Data\Microsoft\Signatures.

When you create a message with that signature, your vCard is inserted as a text file attachment.

The text for the signature will be inserted as usual, and the .vcf file for the vCard will be attached to the message.

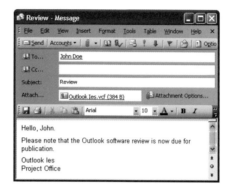

When the message arrives at its destination, your contact details can be added to the addressee's Contact folder or Address Book.

The recipients do not have to be using Outlook to receive and apply the vCard. Here for example, the message is being read using Outlook Express.

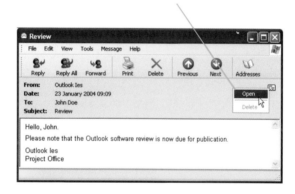

You could save the vCard to disk, as you normally would for other types of file attachment. However, this would not add the details to your Contacts folder. This is why you must open the vCard, then save the details.

6 Open the message, and double-click the vCard file attached.

7 Confirm it is from a trusted source, then select Open it and click OK to view and check the details. Then, save them in the address book or Contacts folder.

Mail merge with contacts

Using Filters (see page 73) you can customize the current view to include a subset of contacts. You can also define just the fields you need, and use Contact fields in current view.

The Distribution Lists (see page 76) in your Contacts folder will not be included in the mail merge.

The selected contact data will be saved in .csv format (comma separated values) so it can be reused or passed on to other Windows applications.

You must map the fields from the Contacts list with the field names that Word expects, for example specifying the field names for the Business Name and Address details.

1 Select Tools from the Menu bar and click Mail Merge.

2 Select All contacts in current view, and All contact fields.

3 Select New document, and name the Contact data file.

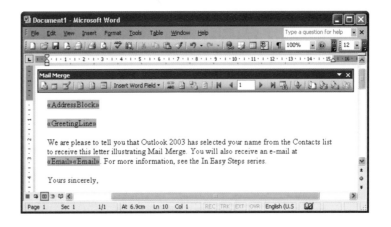

4 Choose Document type as Form Letters, and Merge to a New Document, and click OK to start Word.

5 Use the Mail Merge toolbar or the Mail Merge wizard, and define the form letter using the Contact fields.

6 Word generates a form letter for each of the contacts selected.

Phone dialer

1 Open Contacts, select the entry you want to call and click the AutoDialer button on the Contacts toolbar.

2 Check that the correct phone number is selected and then click Start Call.

If there are numbers you call often, add them to the Speed Dial list, so you can call them without having to select the associated contact entry.

3 To add numbers to the Speed Dial list, click Dialling Options.

4 Type each name, select the number and click Add. Click OK to finish.

You must switch to Contacts to use Speed Dial. You could also select Actions, Call Contact, to use Speed Dial or Redial.

5 Click the AutoDialer down-arrow, select Speed Dial and pick the phone number, or click Redial and select a recent number.

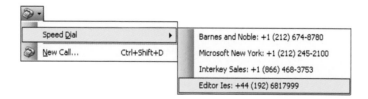

Map contacts

1 Select Contacts, open the particular contact's details and select the address you want to map – Home, Business or Other.

2 Click Display Map of Address on the Standard toolbar, or click Actions, Display Map of Address, on the Menu bar.

3 Assuming that you have an active Internet connection, the appropriate map is displayed.

4 There are options such as travel advice, hotel information, city plans and driving directions. Some of these features are available for US-based addresses only.

Organizing messages

This chapter takes an in-depth look at e-mail productivity
features such as previews, filters and rules, to help you organize
and structure the messages as the volume grows, using backups
and archives for older items.

Covers

Chapter Five

Multiple e-mail accounts

Another way to keep e-mail accounts separate is to have sign-on profiles for all users on your PC. They will logon separately with their own sets of Outlook folders. This provides a higher level of privacy but is a less flexible environment.

There are many situations where you'll have multiple e-mail IDs on your PC. You may sign up with several ISPs, your ISP may offer extra IDs for a shared connection, or you may have an office sign-on and a home sign-on. You could also be sharing your PC with other users.

Outlook can handle all the e-mail accounts, and provides you with facilities to manage and organize the messages you send and receive.

To define an additional account:

1 Select Tools, E-mail Accounts, choose Add a new e-mail account and click Next.

Outlook 2003 supports a number of different server types. You can select from:

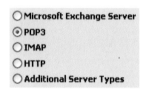

2 Choose the server type for the account and click Next. Then, supply the account details required:

Name/e-mail address   Incoming/outgoing servers

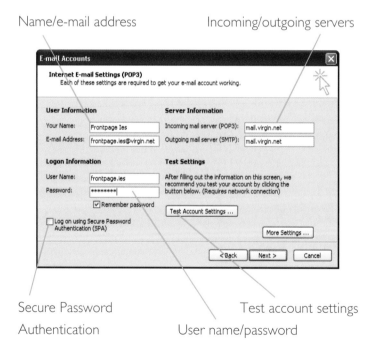

Click Test Account Settings to check that all the entries are correct and to send a test e-mail message to the account you've just added.

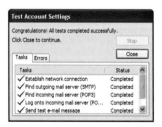

Secure Password Authentication   User name/password   Test account settings

...cont'd

On this panel you can also specify an alternative e-mail address for replies to messages from this account.

Click Outgoing Server and specify the authentication settings required by the ISP.

The connection type will be defined when you set up your connection to the Internet with the ISP (see page 15, Setting up your Internet service).

3 Click More Settings and select the General tab, to provide the name to display on the accounts list.

4 Click the Connection tab and select Connect using my phone line, for a dialup connection, or LAN if you are sharing another PC's connection.

The account will be added to your list of mail services. Repeat the process to add all the accounts that you need to access through the same Outlook configuration. Once they have been defined, you can view the accounts and make changes if required.

5 Select Tools, E-mail Accounts, choose to View or Change existing e-mail accounts, and then click Next to list the accounts.

The accounts can be located at other ISPs and may be for different people but they will all share the same set of Outlook mail folders. Use filters to receive incoming mail in separate folders for each account (see page 92).

Receiving mail

If there are multiple e-mail accounts defined, you will normally receive messages for all the accounts, each time you request mail.

You can change the definition of the e-mail groups (see page 87) including the All Accounts group, so this name may not always mean exactly what the name says.

1 Press the Send/Receive button on the toolbar, and Outlook connects to the Internet and accesses the e-mail accounts.

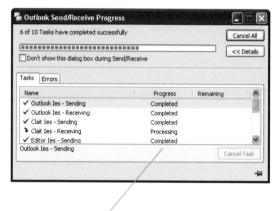

You are able to read mail, but leave it on the server for later collection or deletion (see page 98 for details). This is useful if the main Inbox for an account is on a different PC.

2 All the e-mail accounts are processed in parallel, and Outlook reports progress on the transfers.

3 To send and receive mail from just one account, select Tools, Send/Receive, and then choose the account to process.

When you want to send an e-mail from a specific account, click the Accounts button and select another account to use in place of the default e-mail account.

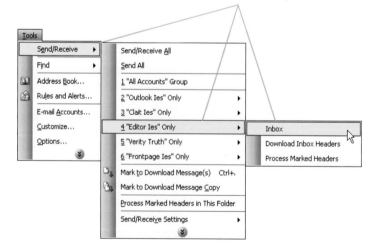

E-mail groups

You can define groups of e-mail accounts and process these accounts together. This process also allows you to rename or redefine the All group.

1 Select Tools, Send/Receive Settings, Define Send/Receive Groups, or press Ctrl+Alt+S, to view or amend account groups.

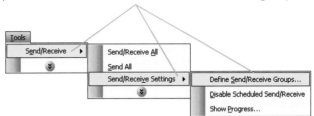

By default, there will be one entry called All Accounts which will contain all the e-mail accounts.

2 Select an existing group and click Edit to make changes, or click New to name and create a new group definition.

Now when you select Tools, Send/Receive you will be able to select one of the new groups of accounts to process.

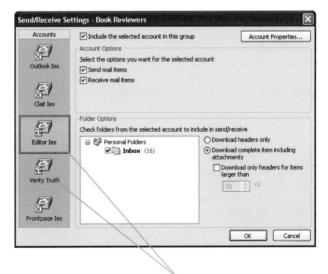

3 Select the accounts that will appear in this group, and the options that you want for each of the accounts.

4 Add any other group definitions that you want.

Managing the Inbox

With many contacts lists, several e-mail addresses and newsletters from Web-based vendors, you'll soon find your Inbox contains a huge list of messages.

Outlook offers numerous ways to manage the problem of an inflated Inbox, including views, filters and folders, but the simplest method may be to sort the messages into a convenient sequence.

1. Open the Inbox and select View, Arrange by, to see a list of the message information fields included in the list.

You can sort only one field at a time, and the order of the list is predetermined. Most will give ascending sequence, but Date and Size will give descending sequence.

2. The current sequence field (Date, by default) will be ticked.

Ascending

Descending

3. Click another field, for example the From field, to make that the sort field, and the Inbox will be resequenced.

Click View, Arrange By, Custom and click the Sort button, and you can select up to four fields for sort sequence, and specify ascending or descending for each.

4. Select Arrange By, Show in Groups, to add headings with item counts, for each value. You can collapse any sublist, to show just the heading.

Sort...   From (ascending)

Click on the [-] button next to the heading to collapse it. The [-] changes to [+]. Click on the [+] button to expand the sublist again.

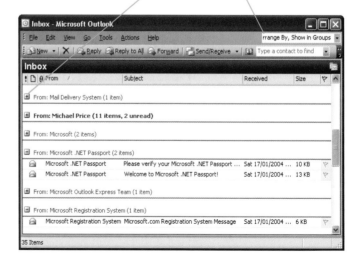

For a temporary resequence, to help you locate a particular message, it may be easier to carry out manual sorts.

For a change of sequence with control over the direction of the sort, simply click the headers in the Inbox list.

5 Click the header to sort the messages in ascending order (e.g. click From to sort by sender).

Outlook will ignore the Re: and Fw: prefixes in the Subject field when sorting.

6 Click the same header again to sort the messages in descending order (e.g. click From to list in reverse order of senders).

When you've finished with manual sorting, click on a header, for example Received, to return the list to Date order, or select View, Arrange By and choose the sort field.

7 Hold down Shift, and click another field for a second level of sort (e.g. Subject, to sort by topic within each sender).

8 You can choose the sort direction by right-clicking the header. This menu also gives you the option to group messages by field.

Inbox Views

There are a number of predefined views that you can select, from the Menu bar or the Navigation Pane.

1. Select View, Arrange By, Current View and either choose one of the six options, or customize the current view, or define your own view.

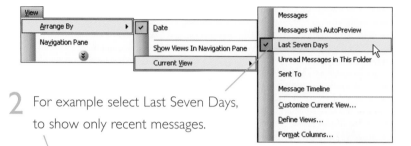

2. For example select Last Seven Days, to show only recent messages.

All the views except Message Timeline are variations of the main message list, and they all display the same set of fields:

- *Importance*
- *Message Type*
- *Attachment Indicator*
- *Flag*
- *Sender*
- *Recipient*
- *Subject*
- *Date Sent*
- *Date Received*

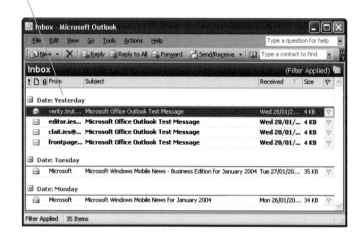

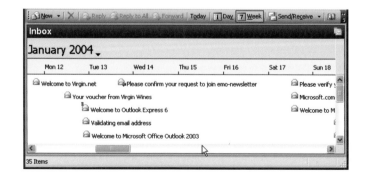

Message Timeline view shows an icon at the message transmission time, with the subject and date. The bars illustrate the delay between sending and receiving messages.

3. Select Message Timeline, and choose the period of time, e.g. 1 Day or 7 Day Week, to show the item chronology.

You can enable views in each of the Navigation Panes individually. The message views can be shown in the Mail, Folder List or Shortcuts panes. Views related to the appropriate Outlook item appear in the Calendar, Contacts, Journal, Notes and Tasks panes.

Adding the Mail Views to the Mail pane will only affect that pane. They will not be added to the Folder List or Shortcuts panes, unless you enable them specifically for each pane.

This list will include any custom views you may have defined (see page 93).

Define Views...

4 If the Navigation Pane (see page 30) is hidden, click View, Navigation Pane to reveal it, then choose the Mail pane.

5 Select View, Arrange By, Show Views in Navigation Pane, and the list of Mail views appears in the pane.

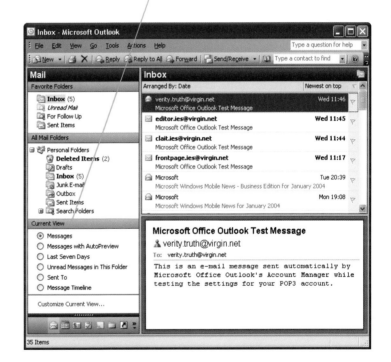

6 Click Customize Current View to add sort fields (see page 88) or to add filters (see page 92).

7 Click View, Reading Pane to change its position (currently at the bottom).

Filter views

1 Select Customize Current View from the Navigation Pane and then click the Filter button.

You can restrict the number of messages that are displayed in your Inbox by specifying values for fields. Filters can be applied to any of Outlook's folders and views, as well as to the Inbox as shown here.

2 Specify the word(s) to search for, e.g. Outlook Web Access, or, to be more precise, "Outlook Web Access".

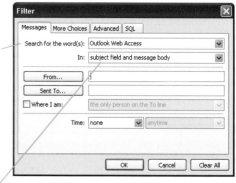

3 Specify where to look – e.g. in subject and text

The More Choices and the Advanced tabs allow you to add further criteria and check the values of additional fields. When your filter includes several criteria, only those messages that meet all of the criteria will appear. The SQL tab allows you to view and change the selection criteria.

of message. Type details in the From or Sent To boxes, if needed. Click OK to apply the filter.

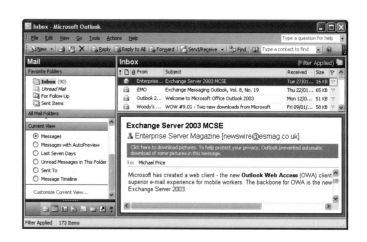

Note that the InfoBar for the message being displayed in the Reading pane says "Outlook prevented automatic download of some pictures in this message." See page 181-186 for more information about this and other Outlook security measures.

173 items in total

Filter... | Off

51 items with words

Filter... | Messages: Containing Outlook Web Access

6 items with phrase

Filter... | Messages: Containing "Outlook Web Access"

Custom views

Another way to manage the Inbox is to create a custom view, or modify an existing view, so only the fields you really need are displayed.

1 Choose the Inbox folder, then select View, Arrange By, Current View, Define Views.

2 Select the current view settings as the starting point, or choose any of the views available, click New, and confirm the view type.

The custom view is called New View by default, though you can change the name, and it will be added to the list of current views.

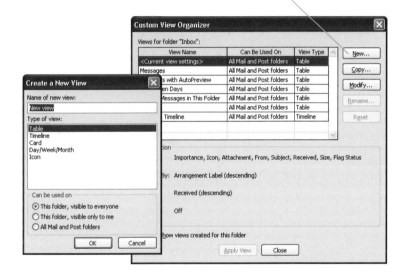

Remove fields that are not required, or change the order of the fields, or add new fields from the list of fields available for Mail items.

3 Customize the new view. For example, click the Fields button and choose which to include or exclude.

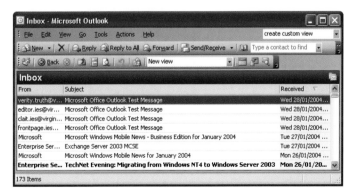

AutoPreview

The Reading Pane provides a quick way to review a single message at a time, without having to actually open it. AutoPreview provides a similar capability for multiple messages.

Open the Inbox and select View, AutoPreview, and the first three lines of each message will be shown below the message headers.

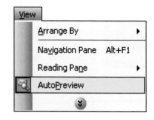

You can use AutoPreview in combination with the Reading Pane, but normally you'd select one of the options as your primary setting.

2 Change the Current View for the Inbox to Messages with Preview, and you'll find that only Unread messages will be auto-previewed.

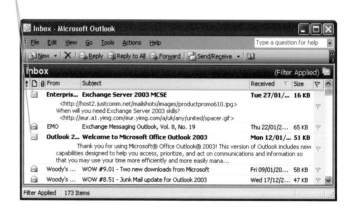

You needn't take up display space for messages that you have already seen. You can select a view that limits the messages previewed.

You set the AutoPreview and Reading Pane options individually for the various message folders, including Inbox, Outbox and Sent.

Adding folders

If it becomes too time-consuming to manage all your messages in the Inbox, you can add more folders and divide up your messages.

The Folder Contains field is preset to the type of Outlook item you are currently viewing, but you can select any type.

I Click the arrow on the New button and click New Folder (or you could select File, New, Folder, or press Ctrl+Shift+E, or right-click an existing folder and select New Folder).

2 Type the name for your new mail folder (e.g. Newsletters). Select the type for the Folder Contents, in this case Mail and Post Items. Specify where the new folder should be created (e.g. in the Inbox).

3 Select the messages that you want to move, and click the Move button.

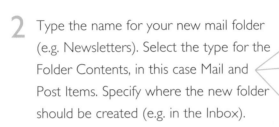

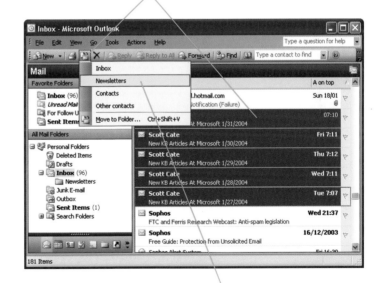

Sort the e-mail messages, then select a view or use a filter to group the messages. This makes it easier to select the messages you want to move.

4 Choose the target folder from the list (Outlook remembers recently used folders) or choose Move to Folder and select the name from the list. Also, if you have the Navigation Pane showing, you can drag and drop messages directly onto the folder.

Organizing by rule

Outlook also applies rules of its own, to detect junk e-mail and divert it to the Junk E-mail folder.

Choose a view or sort sequence that makes the messages easy to find, and select Tools, Organize.

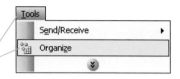

Highlight messages from the particular senders, choose the target folder and click Move to transfer the messages.

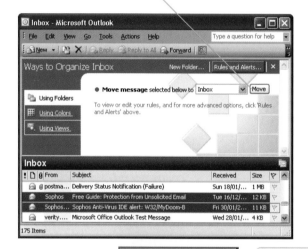

The Organize tool also allows you to choose colors to assign to particular messages in your mail folders.

The wizard gives a list of possible things to check for. Pick a rule template that is close to what you want, or choose Start from a blank rule.

To define the move, click the Rules and Alerts button and click New Rule.

Specify the action, the sender names, and the target folder. You can also specify exceptions, e.g. don't transfer high priority messages.

It makes it easier to select senders if they are defined in your Contacts folder, or you could select messages based on words in the subject.

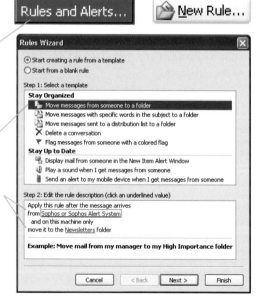

5 When the rule is fully assembled, you can name it, turn it on and choose to apply it to existing messages already in the Inbox.

As a shortcut, you can right-click a message in the Inbox, and select Create Rule, then choose the conditions that apply, and a new rule will be added.

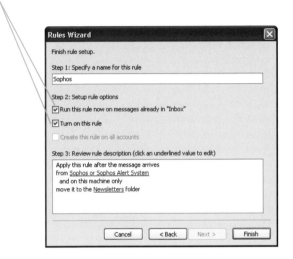

6 Click Finish to set up and apply the rule. It will be added to the end of the existing list of rules.

The rules will be applied whenever a message arrives. To run them explicitly, select Tools, Rules and Alerts, click the Run Rules Now button, choose the specific rules and click Run Now.

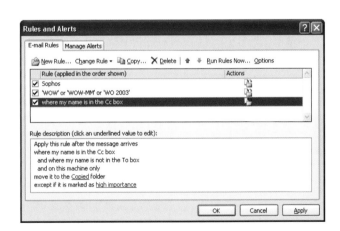

7 Decide the logical order in which to run the rules, e.g. you may want to move newsletters to their folder before checking for messages on which you are copied rather than being a main recipient.

Leaving mail on the server

If you sometimes read your mail from more than one PC, you could end up with your mail spread across several mail boxes. While you can export mail from one system to another a much simpler option is to leave your mail on the server unless you are connecting via your main system (see page 147 for discussion of working away from the office).

Start Outlook on the system where you want to review mail without removing it from the server.

1 Select Tools, E-mail Accounts, and choose the option to View or change existing e-mail accounts.

E-mail Accounts...

2 Select the e-mail account you are working with, click the Change button, and then click the More Settings button.

Change...

More Settings ...

Your ISP may not allow you to save messages on the server. If so, you will see a message box telling you this, when you access your mail with the new setting.

3 Select the Advanced tab and click the Leave a copy of messages on the server box.

4 If appropriate, specify the number of days after which the messages can be removed from the server.

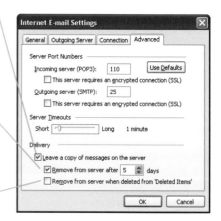

This action could be very useful if you sometimes access your mail from a laptop PC and at other times from a desktop PC.

5 You may choose to have messages deleted from the server when you delete them from your system.

Messages will still be downloaded for viewing, but the originals will be left on the server. You should leave the option unselected on your primary PC. When you sign on from that PC, the messages will be removed from the server when you receive them.

Outlook Calendar

This chapter explores the Outlook Calendar, defining events, appointments and meetings. It also tells you how to use the Calendar to set up and manage projects and meetings, and to share calendar free/busy data over the Internet.

Covers

Chapter Six

The Calendar

The Calendar is a feature of Outlook that has no equivalent in Outlook Express and other e-mail programs. It is designed to keep track of activities and happenings. It gives you a high-level overview of the week or month, also maps the details by the day and the hour, so it is a diary as well as a calendar.

Outlook stores details of appointments and meetings. Activities that last for a whole day or more, such as conferences, holidays and courses, may be treated as an event. Some activities, such as regular meetings or anniversaries, may be repeated.

To display the Calendar:

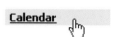

1. Click Calendar on the Navigation Pane, or click the Calendar link on Outlook Today.

An appointment is an activity that involves just yourself. If you need to book resources or to invite other people, it becomes a meeting.

You can also select Go, Calendar from the Menu bar, or press Ctrl+2 to display the Calendar.

The Time bar and the activities are color-coded to classify the time periods as:

- Out of Office
- Busy
- Tentative
- Free

You can also apply color codes to the individual activities.

Date navigator   Time bar   View buttons   Event banner

Calendar pane   Meeting   Appointment   Event   Reminder

2. Click a View button to show the work week, 7-day week or month, or select View, Task Pad to see a summary of tasks.

Adding an event

You'll probably want to start by transferring your pocket diary entries, putting down major events such as vacations and conferences, or special events such as birthdays and anniversaries. To add an event to your Calendar:

1 Open Calendar and select Actions, New All Day Event (or in day/week/month view, double-click the date heading for the day).

2 Type a brief description for the event, specify the location, and specify the start date (and end date for multi-day events).

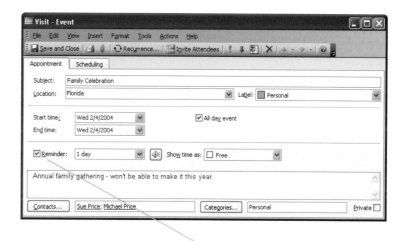

3 Click the box to request a reminder (minutes, hours or days) before the event. You can also set a priority code for the event.

4 Show your time as Free or Out of the Office, and label (color code) the event as appropriate.

5 Add a longer description, contacts and category details. Click Save and Close to record the details for the event.

Adding national holidays

Adding entries one at a time can become tedious, so Outlook provides a way to add holidays en bloc.

Calendar Options also allow you to specify the length of the work day, the scope of the work week and the year start (e.g. Jan 1, or first full week.)

Select Tools, Options, and then click the Preferences tab. Click the Calendar Options button, and then click the Add Holidays button.

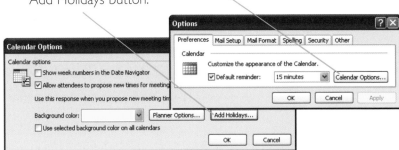

Choose the required location and click OK to add the national holidays.

You can add holidays and special days from more than one location, and there are also specific sets of religious holidays.

The holidays are added to the headers for the respective dates and are shown as one-day events. You can edit the events list (see page 103) to remove duplicate entries or unnecessary items.

To view the holiday list, change the current view for the Calendar to Events. You'll see holidays for the years 2003–2007. You can add to the group or create your own groups (see page 104). An alternative way to define holidays is to specify them as annually recurring events (see page 107).

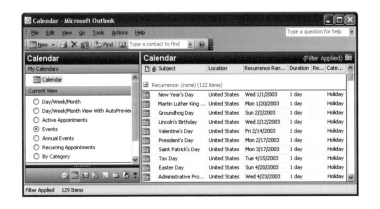

Editing the events list

To make it easier to edit the events list, sort by clicking the column headers. For example, sort by location within subject.

1 Select one or more events that are not required and press the Delete key to transfer them to the Deleted Items folder.

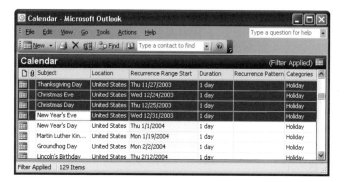

2 Hold down the Shift key as you press Delete, to permanently delete the selected items.

If you open an event and change the date without making a copy, the original event will be lost.

3 Select an entry and click Edit, Copy and then Edit, Paste to make a duplicate. Double-click the new event to adjust the dates, e.g. to add Christmas Day 2006, 2007, etc.

If the reset button is grayed, the view selected has not been modified, or it is a custom view (which has no original setting).

4 If you change view settings – e.g. expand column widths, or sort the entries – return to the original settings with View, Current View, Define Views. Select the view, click the Reset button and confirm you do want to reset the view.

Custom holiday list

To include all the special days you need in your calendar, modify the Outlook Holidays list.

Previous versions of Outlook stored the holiday lists in a file called Outlook.txt. In Outlook 2003 the file is called Outlook.hol.

The format for the entries in the plain text Outlook.hol file is as follows:

[Description] nnn
Event name,yyyy/mm/dd
(with no spaces between the name and the date)

Make sure that the count nnn matches the number of entries, or Outlook may ignore some of your additions.

You can leave out lists for locations that you don't use, but keep the backup copy of Outlook.hol, just in case.

1 Select Start, Search, Files and folders to find the Outlook.hol file. Select File, Open Containing Folder, and make a backup copy of the file.

2 Right-click the file icon and select Open With, NotePad. Modify existing lists you use, or add new lists of your particular events, using existing lists as a guide. Save the modified file.

3 Select Tools, Options, Calendar Options, Add Holidays. Your existing entries will be recognized and selected. Select your new entries and click OK.

4 If you didn't change the existing lists, click No so that you do not re-install them into the calendar.

If you have modified an existing list and do need to re-install it, delete the associated events from the calendar first, or you may end up with some duplicate events.

Scheduling appointments

You can schedule an appointment in your calendar to remind yourself that there is something you have to do or a place where you have to be. This can also signal to anyone with access to your calendar that you may be unavailable at the time concerned.

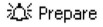
1 Open the Calendar and click the New button, or double-click a time slot (in day or work week view), or select Action, New Appointment, or press Ctrl+N.

2 Enter the Subject and select the Location from the list, or type in a new location.

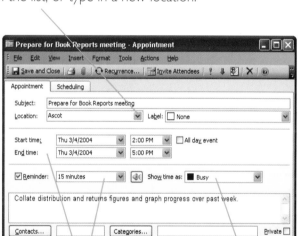

3 Specify the start time and the end time (or duration), and set a reminder period.

4 Select a color code, and mark the period as Busy time or Out of Office.

5 Type a more detailed description, add associated contact names, set a category, or mark Private, as appropriate. Click Save and Close, to add the details to the Calendar.

Rescheduling

1 In day or work week view, point to the item to be moved. When the pointer becomes a 4-way arrow, left-click to drag the item.

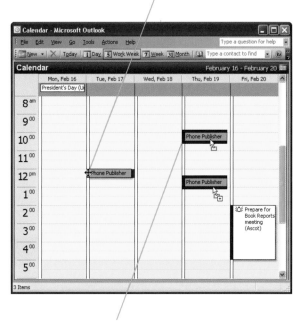

2 Drag to the required time and day, and release the mouse button to drop the item in its new time slot.

3 In week or month view, select and drag the item as described above, and drop it into a new day slot, to change the date.

4 Alternatively, you can change the day and the month if you drop the item onto a new date on the date navigator.

Recurring activities

When an appointment or other activity happens on a regular basis, you can add multiple entries into your calendar with one Outlook operation.

1 Open the Calendar to select the item, and double-click to open it and display the current details.

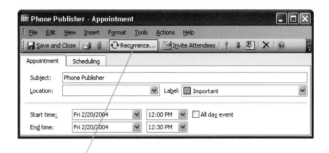

2 Click the Recurrence button. By default the appointment will be repeated indefinitely, once every week, at the same time and day as the original.

You can specify a monthly pattern selecting, for example, the third Friday of each month, or you can choose a yearly pattern.

3 You could choose to schedule the appointment several times a week.

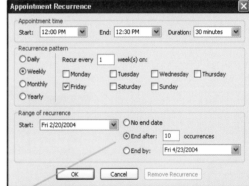

4 The repeats can be limited by total number or by a cut-off date.

When you double-click a recurring entry, you'll be asked if you want to edit details for the particular instance, or the whole series (the pattern).

5 In the day and week views, the recurring entries appear with a circle symbol ↻ to indicate that they are repeated events.

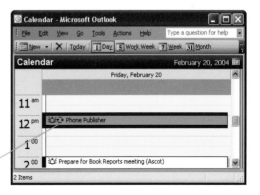

Meetings

The definition of a meeting is quite simple: it is an appointment that involves at least one other calendar as well as your own. In practice, a meeting can become quite a complex affair. You have to consider not only the availability of other people, but also the allocation of meeting rooms and of equipment such as projectors or video recorders, and you have to keep everyone informed when the details change.

It is useful to know how Outlook handles meetings, even if you don't have to plan them. It will help you to understand what is involved when you are the recipient of message requests, for meetings that other people set up.

This can all be done manually, with phone calls or e-mail messages to the attendees or the persons responsible for booking the room and equipment. However, Outlook includes the facilities for fully managing meetings. Meeting requests and replies keep attendees informed. Required resources can be managed similarly, with special e-mail addresses which respond to requests based on the booking schedules.

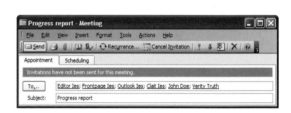

Outlook provides two ways to share information about free and busy times. Users can give one another access to the contents of their calendars (see page 109), or they can publish details on a file server or Internet site (see page 110).

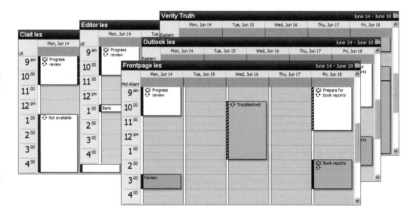

To allow you to plan a meeting without having to wait for responses, it would be useful to see the schedules for all the attendees (and for any required resources) so you can choose a suitable date and time to avoid or minimize conflicts. Outlook gives you access to this data, and sends out meeting requests to the attendees and the resource contacts.

Sharing calendars

If you use Exchange Server for your e-mail, your Outlook folders are stored on the server, and you can allow other users to access your calendar, and access the calendars of other users.

Note that Share My Calendar does not appear unless you are using an Exchange Server e-mail account.

1. From the Navigation Pane, click the Calendar button, and then click Share My Calendar.

2. Allow anyone on the same server to access your calendar, or specify the users who are permitted access.

3. Click Open a Shared Calendar, and type the name, or click Name and pick an entry from the address book.

The selected calendars will open alongside your calendar. You can view up to 30 calendars side-by-side.

You can achieve a similar effect even if you are using Outlook without Exchange Server.

If you are sharing an Outlook system with other users, you can each use a subfolder of the Calendar to store your schedules, then you can open these subfolders side-by-side.

If your associates are using different systems, they can Export their calendars periodically, and you can Import them as subfolders to your calendar.

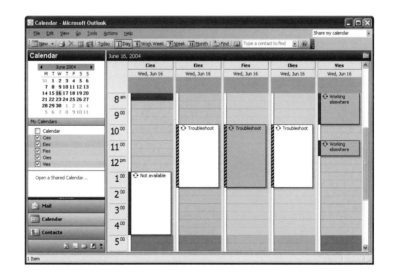

4. When you scroll the display or change the date, all the calendars move in sync, so you can check availability for meetings.

Reporting free/busy time

Ideally, one person would be designated to set up the meeting, using the combined availability data, and the AutoPick function, to schedule times that avoid calendar conflicts.

If you and your associates share access to a file server on a local area network or to pages on a Web server, each of you can publish the details of your calendar.

1 Select Tools, Options, then click the Preferences tab, and select Calendar Options.

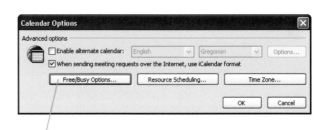

Calendar Options...

The maximum time between updates is 60 minutes. With a slower speed or dialup connection to the Internet, you may decide to disable this feature except when you specifically choose to update the data.

2 Select Free/Busy Options from the Advanced Options section. Choose how many months of free/busy data to send to the server, and decide how frequently to refresh.

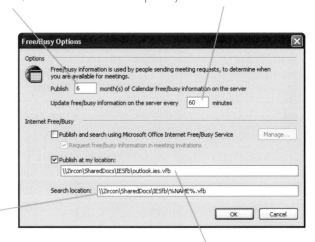

If you are going to be planning meetings, specify the Search Location also.
This is the same as the file name, but with the user name replaced by the variable %NAME%, representing any user name.

3 Specify the location to store the data, on a local drive, a network drive or a Web server. The file name should include the user name part of your e-mail address (the part before the @ sign). The file type for free/busy information is .vfb.

4 Outlook will refresh the free/busy information automatically at the requested interval. To make an immediate update, select Tools, Send/Receive, Free/Busy Information.

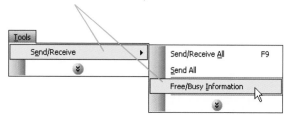

5 Outlook will transfer the information from your calendar and tell you the status of the operation when it completes.

Note that only information from your main calendar folder will be transferred to the storage location.

6 From now on, when you plan a meeting (see page 118) the availability for attendees who have published their free/busy data will be used to help schedule the meeting.

There will be no free/busy data for attendees who have not posted data, or for attendees where you specify an e-mail address that is not the same as the address used for the data storage.

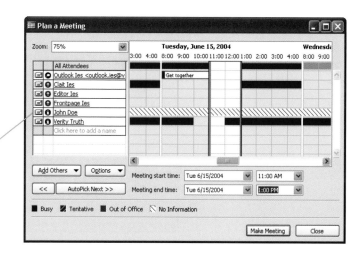

Internet free/busy service

For those who don't have access to a shared drive, Microsoft offers an Internet Free/Busy service. You and the users must obtain the Microsoft Passport form of identification, which consists of your e-mail address plus a password.

1 The users must each select Tools, Options, click the Preferences tab, select Calendar Options, and click Free/Busy Options.

2 Choose how many months of free/busy data to send to the service, and decide how frequently to refresh.

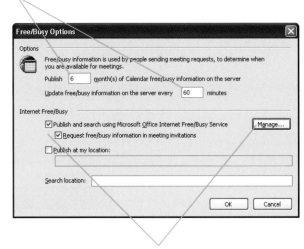

You must sign on to Microsoft Passport, and change your profile to share your e-mail address (if it is not already shared). You also need to have Internet Explorer 5.0 installed, but it doesn't have to be used as your browser.

3 Select the Internet Free/Busy service, for publishing and requesting free/busy data, and click the Manage button.

You can choose to make your data available to all members of the service. This saves entering specific e-mail addresses but leaves you with no effective control over who sees the information.

4 Provide the e-mail addresses for the users who will be allowed to access your availability data.

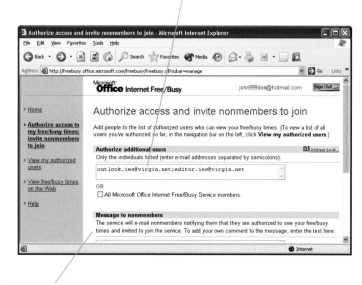

When you view the availability data at the Microsoft Web site, it is presented in blocks of eight hours at a time. You can view the data for any members that have authorized you explicitly or that have authorized service members in general., as long as you know the e-mail address used to register the data.

5 The service recognizes those who are already members of the service, and sends e-mails to invite non-members to join up.

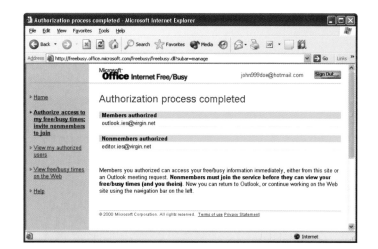

6 You can view free/busy time at the Web site, or access it in Outlook when you schedule meetings (see page 118).

Converting appointments

1 Select Calendar and double-click the appointment to view it.

2 Click the Scheduling tab and click Add Others to select required or optional attendees from Contacts.

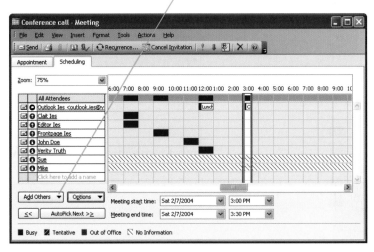

3 Select the Appointment tab, make any required changes to details such as location, description or category, then press Send.

4 Meeting request e-mails will be sent to each of the attendees, so they can reply, and add the details to their own calendars.

Meeting requests

 Meeting request

 Accepted

 Tentative

 Declined

 Users with older versions of Outlook, or with other PIM applications will be able to respond to message requests, but participants using e-mail systems such as Outlook Express that do not support the vCalendar interface will not. You should invite such users with an ordinary e-mail message.

 The meeting time shown on the request will be according to the participant's time zone. The 3pm Eastern meeting will be shown as 18:00 (6pm) mid-Atlantic, or 20:00 (8pm) in the UK.

 The meeting will be added to your calendar, and a response will be sent to the originator. Put a comment on the response if you wish.

1 A participant receives the meeting request, and replies by clicking the appropriate response, e.g. Accept, Tentative or Decline.

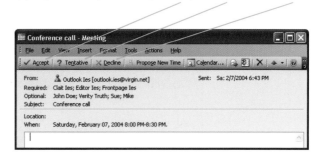

2 You can reply to a meeting request without even opening the message, if you use the Reading Pane.

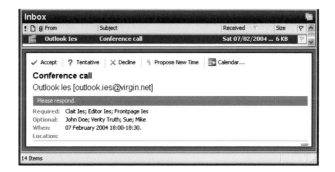

3 As responses are made, the requests are removed from the Inbox, and messages are sent to the originator for processing.

4 Open any of the responses, and you'll see any comments that have been added, plus a summary of responses so far.

The originator sees the meeting time in the local time zone, even though the participants in other locations see different times. Outlook automatically adjusts the times to suit the viewer's location.

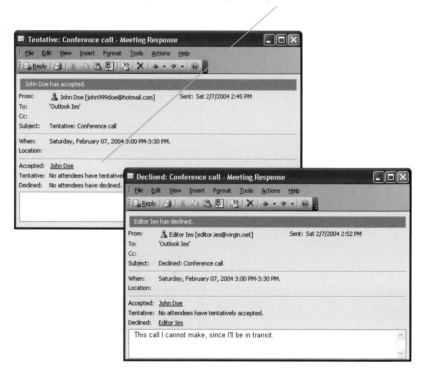

5 The responses are also added to the meeting details stored in the Calendar, as you'll see if you open the meeting entry.

The Tracking page shows the current status of responses from the participants who have accepted, tentatively accepted or declined the invitation to the meeting.

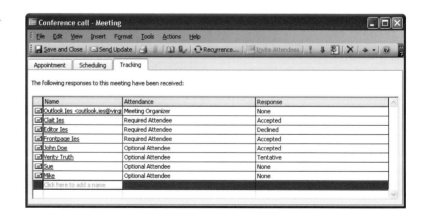

Changing meetings

You may need to change the details when you receive the invitations and receive responses.

1 Find the meeting in your calendar, double-click the meeting to open it, and select the Appointment tab.

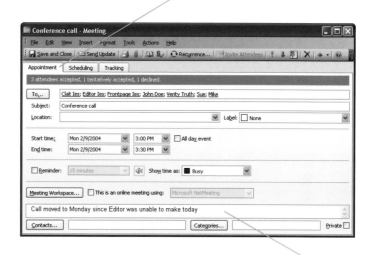

If you change the meeting details to add more attendees, you should Forward a copy of the meeting request to the new attendees, to avoid having duplicate requests sent to all the original attendees.

2 Make required changes, e.g. the scheduled date, add a note to the description if appropriate, then click Save and Close.

There is a dynamic link between the Tracking page and the responses. When you open a response, it will pick up the latest status. If you reschedule the meeting then look at one of the responses, you'll see that the status has been updated.

3 Click Yes to send the updated meeting request to all on the original distribution list. They can then confirm their acceptances.

You'll get a warning whenever you make changes, even if you don't open the meeting notice – for example, if you select the meeting and press Delete to cancel it.

Planning meetings

Outlook provides a structured approach towards setting up a meeting, helping you ensure that you get everything right first time, so you don't have to make changes.

1. Open the Calendar, select Actions from the Menu bar and click Plan a Meeting.

2. Select Add Others, Add from Address Book, and select entries from your contacts list – attendees and resources.

Press Options and choose settings such as Show Only Working Hours and Show Calendar Details.

3. Set the duration of the meeting and click the AutoPick button to select the next (or previous) start time that fits with schedules for the attendees and resources that you selected.

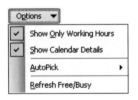

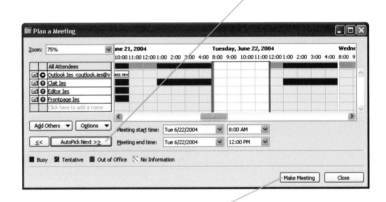

4. Select Make Meeting, specify the Subject, Location and details of the meeting, then press Send to issue invitations.

See page 110 for methods of reporting and sharing free/busy time on a shared drive, or over the Internet.

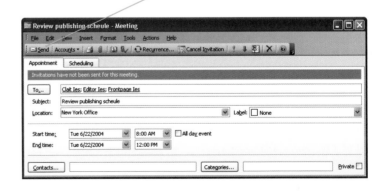

Task Manager

This chapter explores the Outlook Task Manager, showing how tasks are created, updated and assigned to others. It shows you how to keep everyone informed, and looks at the role of the TaskPad and the Today tasks.

Covers

Chapter Seven

Setting up a task list

A Task is a personal or work-related errand that you want to track through to completion. It can happen once, or be repeated on some sort of regular basis. You can perform it yourself or assign it to someone else.

The Task folder in Outlook operates as a task list manager. In it, you can enter a list of everything that you must do to complete the job or project that you have in hand. The list could include prompts to make phone calls, to prepare meetings, to write letters or reports, to set up travel arrangements – in fact, anything that you need to do!

For each task you can specify details such as the subject, date required, priority and current status. You can also set reminders, as you do for meetings and appointments, so that you are warned when the critical time approaches.

As usual, Outlook provides a number of ways to open the folder, so you can use the method that best suits your particular setup.

To open the Task folder and enter a task:

1. Click Tasks in the Navigation Pane or click the title in the Outlook Today window (or pick Go, Tasks, or press Ctrl+4).

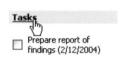

If you just enter the task titles, Outlook sets the due date to None, and you create a useful to-do checklist for your project.

2. To create an entry in the list, click on the new task line, type the item title in the subject box, and press Enter.

3. The new entries get entered at the top of the list, but you can click the heading to sort tasks by subject or due date.

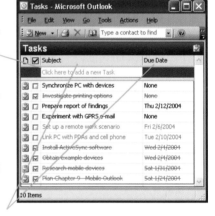

The default is the Simple view which shows the task title and the due date. You can switch to the Detailed List view to add status, percentage complete and category data (see page 122).

4. You can type in the due date or click the down-arrow and select the date from the calendar displayed, or click the Today button or the None button.

Task details

 Describe the task more fully, when you create it, or when more information becomes available.

1 Click the New Task button on the toolbar or double-click the New task line, or double-click an existing task entry.

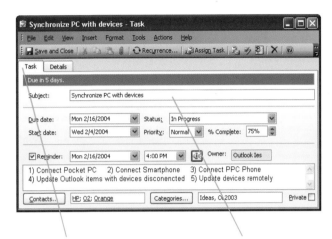

 Put None, if the date is not yet known, and complete the details later.

 The reminder date and time can be used as a prompt for starting or for finishing a task. You can also select a suitable .wav sound file to play alongside the warning message.

2 Select the Task tab and type in the task Subject. Specify the due date and start date (click the down-arrow for a calendar to help find dates).

3 Choose the current status from the list. This entry should be reviewed and amended as the status changes.

 Priority defaults to Normal, or you can select Low or High for the task.

4 Type in the % Complete to show the current position, or click the arrows for 25% increments.

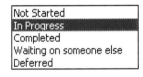

5 Specify the task description, contact names and the category code and update these values whenever appropriate.

6 Select the Details tab to provide further information including the actual completion date, and the billing data (see page 128).

Viewing the task list

Select View from the Menu bar, click Current View, and select which view to make current.

The Simple List view shows the task subjects and completion dates, and acts as a quick overview of the status of the project. You can double-click any task to open it.

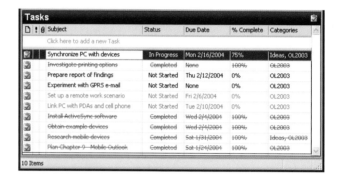

The Detailed List view adds more information, so you can sort the tasks by status or category, etc. by just clicking the relevant heading. It is a good place to update the status and completion data, without opening each individual task.

You can view selective lists, e.g. the Active tasks which are those not yet completed. Other filtered views show tasks for the next week, by responsible person, overdue, or completed.

All the task views are lists, except for the final view – the timeline. Here you can get an idea of the relative timings of the tasks, to identify potential conflicts or dependencies.

Tasks are tracked by whole days, so a task that starts and ends on the same day does not have any duration on the timeline.

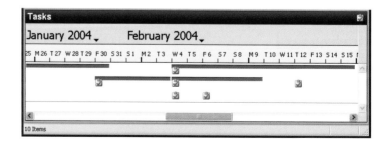

Working with tasks

Reminders only make sense if you frequently sign on to Outlook (or at least once a day).

As your project continues, reference the task list to remind yourself what needs to be done next, and update the entries to reflect progress. You may simply tick off activities when they are completed, or you can track their intermediate status and update the amount completed.

As the completion date for a task approaches, you get a reminder (if specified). You are also warned if the due date passed without the task being marked complete.

When you get two or more reminders at one time, you can click Dismiss All to dismiss them all at once.

A dismissed reminder is completely removed, and will never reappear, so you may prefer to specify an appropriate delay. This may be a period of five minutes, or up to two weeks.

There are several possible actions to take:

1 Select several items and click the Open button to update them, or the Dismiss button to cancel them.

| 5 minutes |
| 10 minutes |
| 15 minutes |
| 30 minutes |
| 1 hour |
| 2 hours |
| 4 hours |
| 8 hours |
| 0.5 days |
| 1 day |
| 2 days |
| 3 days |
| 4 days |
| 1 week |
| 2 weeks |

2 Right-click a task to open it, or to mark it as completed.

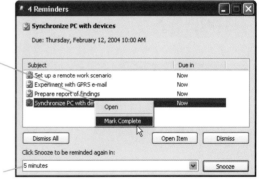

3 Select a delay time, and click Snooze to postpone all of the selected reminders.

You don't have to wait for reminders, to process the tasks in your list. Click one or more tasks in the list and right-click the selection.

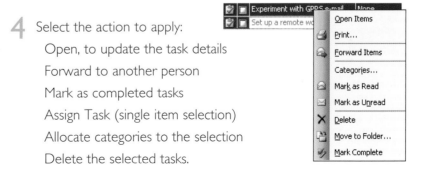

See page 124 for details of task assignments, and page 126 for status reports on assigned tasks.

4 Select the action to apply:
   Open, to update the task details
   Forward to another person
   Mark as completed tasks
   Assign Task (single item selection)
   Allocate categories to the selection
   Delete the selected tasks.

Assigning tasks

You don't necessarily complete all the tasks in your folder yourself. You can define tasks as part of a project and then transfer them for someone else to complete. That person becomes the new owner, if the task assignment is accepted, and will send you status updates and notice of completion.

You can right-click the task in the list and choose Assign Task.

1 Open the task and click Assign Task (which then changes to show Cancel Assignment).

2 Specify the name of the new owner of the task, and add an explanatory note.

Outlook will switch off any reminders that were set for the original task assignment.

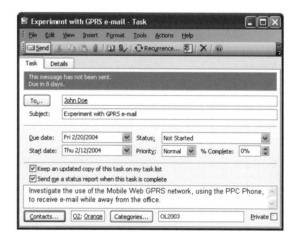

If you do change your mind before the message leaves the Outbox, you can cancel the assignment.

3 Leave a copy of the task in your folder if you want to keep track of the status. Then click Send, to e-mail the prospective new task owner.

4 The icon for the task in the list shows that it has been handed-on to someone else.

Once you've assigned a task, you can no longer make changes to the task definitions, even if you have not yet received a reply.

5 You can open the task, get status reports and updates, but you can't make changes.

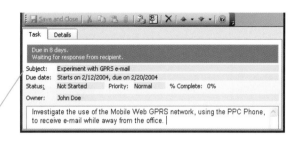

The assignee can respond to the task request from the Reading Pane, without opening the e-mail message.

Task assignments arrive as normal mail in the Inbox. When the message is opened, the prospective owner takes the appropriate action:

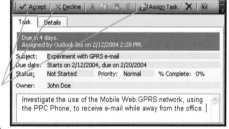

6 Accept the task and become the new owner, Decline the task, or Assign it to someone else.

You can edit the response before it is sent, if you need to qualify your answer or add more information.

The task will be moved to the Task, Deleted or Outbox folder as appropriate and a message will be sent to inform the original owner of the action taken.

Any declined tasks will be reassigned to the original owner. If the proposed owner does not reply, the task will be left in limbo. One way to claim it back is to create an unassigned copy (see step 7 on page 129).

7 When the replies are received, the original owner's task list will be updated to show the latest status of the tasks after the assignment request has been accepted.

Updating an assigned task

When the new owner makes changes to the task details, the original owner receives an update message, and Outlook will automatically adjust the details in the task list.

1 Open the task and make the appropriate changes, amending the Status, % Complete, and other fields as required.

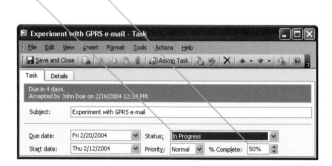

The changes are automatically sent as an update notice to the original owner, as long as a copy of the task was left in that person's task list when the task was assigned (see page 124).

At any stage, the new owner can send a status report to the original owner or to anyone else interested in the task.

2 Select Actions, Send Status Report to create a status report.

3 Outlook will generate a report with the latest values for the fields in the task record. You can add your comments to this report.

By default, the original owner will receive a status report, but you can add e-mail IDs for anyone interested in the particular task.

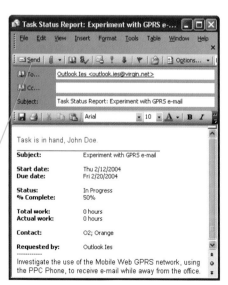

4 Click Send to add the status report to the Outbox for later transmission.

*Outlook will
delete the task-
related messages
when the update
has been applied,
except in the case of Task
Complete messages, which are
retained in the Inbox.*

5 Acceptance messages and status reports appear in the Inbox but get automatically processed and applied to the Task folder. Status update reports appear as normal messages.

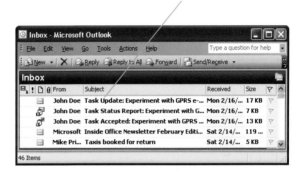

*It isn't necessary
to own a task to
forward it, or to
request updates
on its progress.*

You can send a copy of the task to anyone interested in the project, to add to their own task folders.

*Drag any
additional tasks
from the task list
to the text box of
the message you
are creating.*

6 Open the task, and select Actions, Forward. A new message form opens, and the task becomes an attachment.

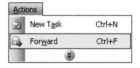

7 Specify e-mail addresses for the recipients, type any additional notes, then click Send.

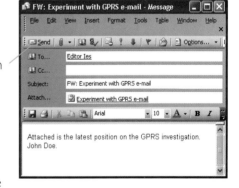

*You must open
the message and
then open the
attachment, in
order to save it as
a task in the task folder.*

8 The recipient should open the attached task, then click Save and Close to add it in the Task folder.

Keeping more information

For most tasks, all the data fields you need can be found on the Task tab of the input sheet. For simple tasks, just the title and the completion date will suffice.

If the tasks are large or complex, you may need to record more detailed statistics, and keep track of the time spent on the task, the people you deal with and the expenses involved. This data becomes essential when you assign tasks to people and account for their time. To enter the data, open the task and select the Details tab. You can specify the following fields:

Type the initial letter of the time period: m (minute), h (hour) d (day) or w (week), and Outlook completes the word. See the opposite page for the definition of the day and week for tasks.

Actual work: the measured work effort to date, or in total for completed tasks, in hours, days or weeks. Note that those neat graphic symbols on the Task input sheet have no function – they are just decorative.

1 Total work: the estimated work effort to complete the task, in minutes, hours, days or weeks.

2 Date completed: the final completion date for the task, which may be different from Due date.

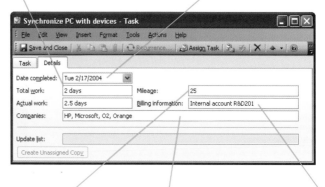

3 Mileage: space for mileage or other travel costs and factors, entered as free-form text.

4 Billing information: time or account details for work related to the task, entered as free-form text.

5 Companies: Names of companies and people associated with the task. This field is plain text only, and does not make use of the address book or contacts list.

...cont'd

The Update List field and the Create Unassigned Copy button are used only with assigned or reassigned tasks.

6 Update list: the people who keep an updated copy in their task lists. This entry is maintained by Outlook.

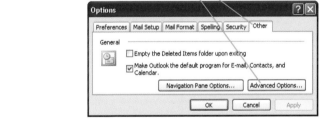

To assign a task to several people at once, make copies with similar names rather than reassigning the same task.

7 Create Unassigned Copy: this button is used by the original owner to copy a task and reassign it to another person.

Hours, days and weeks

When you enter a duration in the total work or actual work fields, Outlook assumes hours, unless you specify the unit as minutes, days or weeks. No other units are allowed. Outlook converts the values to days or weeks, using factors of 8 hours per day and 40 hours per week. To change these factor values:

The Appearance options section in the Advanced Options is intended to control the Date Navigator, but also includes these time-period definitions.

1 Select Tools from the Menu bar, select Options, Other tab, and then Advanced Options.

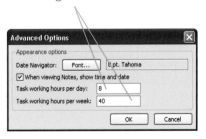

Set the number of hours per day or per week to suit your working practises, or to fit in with a part-time project.

2 Adjust the number of hours in the working day, and the number of hours in the working week.

Calendar TaskPad

The TaskPad in Calendar acts as a mini Task Manager, where you can create and update tasks, just as you do in the Task List views.

1 Click Calendar on the Navigation Pane, or select Go Calendar, and ensure that the Day/Week/Month view is selected.

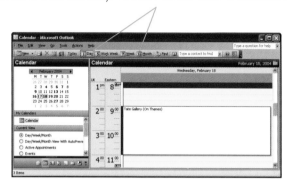

2 Select View, TaskPad to display the Date Navigator and TaskPad together. This turns off the Date Navigator in the Navigation Pane (if displayed).

Add new tasks or change the details for existing tasks. Double-click the task title to open it and change further details.

Changes or additions that you make in the TaskPad will also show up in the full Task list.

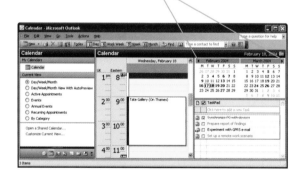

You can display all the tasks in the list, or just today's tasks, and distinguish between active, completed and overdue tasks. You can make changes to your task list straight from TaskPad.

3 Right-click the TaskPad area to shows the options.

4 Select TaskPad View, to choose which tasks you want to display.

Outlook Today tasks

1   On the Outlook Today window, select Customize Outlook Today.

2   All Tasks shows complete and incomplete tasks. Today's Tasks shows the tasks due today, plus any overdue tasks, and (optionally) those with no due date specified.

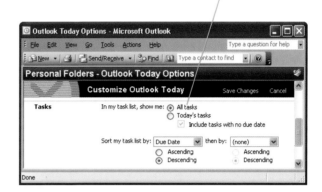

3   Overdue tasks, past the due date without being marked complete, show in red. Click in the box to update the task status. A tick marks it as completed (the title is struck through to emphasize this). Blank means that the task is incomplete.

Scheduling task time

When you have defined a task, you can use the entry in the Task list to help you to set aside time in your Calendar to review progress or complete the task.

1 Select the task from the Task list and drag it over the Calendar icon on the Navigation Pane.

2 Release the task and the Appointment form opens automatically.

The diary entry will be set as an appointment with details of the task appended. It will have the current day specified, but you can change the time, date or type of meeting to suit your needs. For example, you could set up a recurring project review meeting.

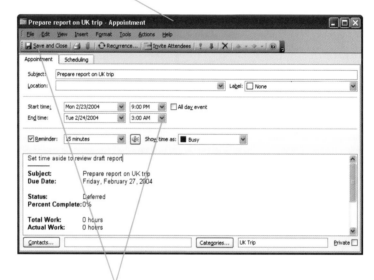

3 Specify the date, start time etc. then press Save and Close.

You can also drag tasks from the Calendar TaskPad and drop them onto a day in the Calendar view, or onto a date in the Date Navigator. This will open the appointments form, so you can specify the start date, time and other appointment details.

Journal and Notes

Outlook keeps track of your communications, whatever form they take, using the Journal. It also tracks activities by contacts. If these records don't tell you all you need to know about your projects, you can use Notes to complete the details.

Covers

Chapter Eight

Configuring the Journal

The Journal is a folder within Outlook which records the times of meetings, phone calls, message responses and other activities related to your project. It is really a kind of log book, since it deals with the start and stop times and other relevant (if minor) details of the item being recorded, rather than with the actual contents.

You don't have to supply all these details yourself since it will automatically record Outlook items, including e-mail messages, meetings and tasks, for the contacts you specify. It can also record the work you do on Microsoft Office items, including databases, spreadsheets, reports, presentations and documents.

For items/contacts that are not being automatically logged, you can add details manually. This means that you can include other types of activities or work items, not just the ones Outlook knows about.

To specify the criteria and start recording:

Journal starts out inactive, and doesn't even appear on the Navigation Pane. To display it, right-click a button and select Navigation Pane Options,

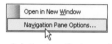

then click the box for Journal.

I Select Journal from the Navigation Pane and open the Journal.

2 If the Journal is already active, but you want to change the criteria, select Tools from the Menu bar, then Options and select the Preferences tab. Then, click Journal Options.

If the Journal is inactive at this time, Outlook offers to turn it on. Click No to view existing Journal entries, or click Yes to display Journal Options.

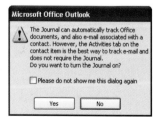

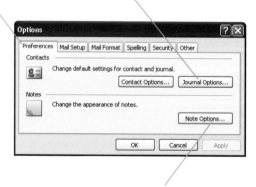

3 This panel provides access to the Note Options (see page 144), as well as the Journal Options.

...cont'd

Set up or change the items and contacts that are recorded in the Journal.

4 Select the item types you want to track, and the contacts for whom you want these records kept.

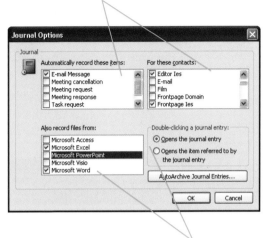

5 Choose the types of Office documents you want to track and record in the Journal, and specify the action to take when you double-click one of the Journal entries.

By default, AutoArchive will run every 14 days, and will process items that are more than six months old. You can set different criteria or skip archive altogether for particular folders.

6 Click AutoArchive Journal Entries in the above dialog box to show the properties which specify when older entries are archived or deleted.

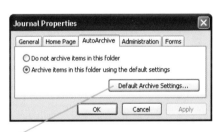

7 Click the Default Archive Settings button to review and adjust default settings.

Viewing Journal entries

As with all the Outlook functions, you can change the manner in which items are displayed.

1 Select View, Arrange By, Current View.

This groups the entries in a timeline view, as do the By Contact and By Category views. You can specify a range of a day, a week, or a month at a time.

2 Select the view you want to use, for example By Contact, or define a custom view.

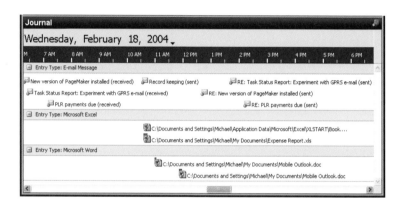

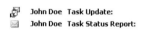

When you log e-mails, ordinary messages are tracked, but you won't see special messages such as task updates or meeting requests, unless you explicitly request that type of information.

The items can also be displayed in a list or table format, with columns for the identifying icon, the entry type, the subject, the start time, the duration, the contact and the category of the item.

You can filter the list to restrict the entries, and make it easier to spot the records you are interested in. To apply a filter to the Journal, choose the view. Click View, Current View, Customize Current View and click the Filter button.

3 Select View, Current View, and choose Entry List (or Last Seven Days, to see only the more recent entries).

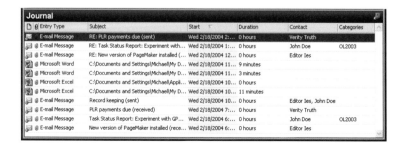

Journal icons and meanings

 Journal uses Outlook icons with a clock symbol, to identify the types of items shown in the timeline views and in the item lists.

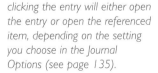 *Icons similar to these (but without the clock symbol) are also used for the item lists in the Calendar, Contacts, E-mail and Tasks views.*

 The attachment is a shortcut to the external file that the journal entry records. Double-clicking the entry will either open the entry or open the referenced item, depending on the setting you choose in the Journal Options (see page 135).

Icon	Item	Meaning
	Conversation	Record of informal meeting
	Document	Manual record or nonspecific file type
	E-mail Message	Standard e-mail message sent or received
	Fax	Fax message sent or received
	Letter	Letter sent or received
	Meeting	Scheduled meeting held
	Meeting cancellation	Scheduled meeting cancelled
	Meeting request	Request for scheduled meeting
	Meeting response	Response to meeting request
	Microsoft Access	Database activity or shortcut
	Microsoft Excel	Spreadsheet activity or shortcut
	Microsoft PowerPoint	Presentation activity or shortcut
	Microsoft Visio	Visio activity or shortcut
	Microsoft Word	Word activity or shortcut
	Note	Record of activity or event
	Phone call	Record of phone call date, time and duration
	Remote session	Record of remote session
	Task	Record of planned or assigned task
	Task request	Request to carry out task
	Task response	Response to task request
	Attachment	Paperclip indicates entry with attachment

Manual recording

To record a Journal entry for any Outlook item:

A shortcut to the item is added to the Journal entry. This may become invalid if the item gets moved or deleted later.

1 Open the folder that contains the entry you wish to track.

2 Select the item and drag it to Journal on the Navigation Pane.

The Subject, Entry type, Contact, and Company boxes and other data are extracted from the item. You can supplement or amend any of this information.

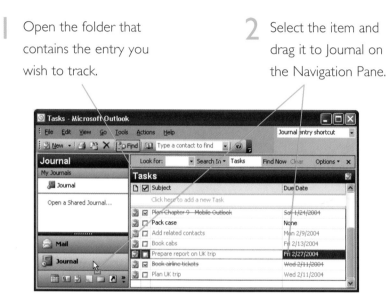

3 A Journal entry opens. Amend it as required then click Save and Close to add the record to the Journal.

When you make a phone call or hold a meeting with clients, create a Journal entry to record the event. Use the Start Timer and Pause Timer buttons to record the duration.

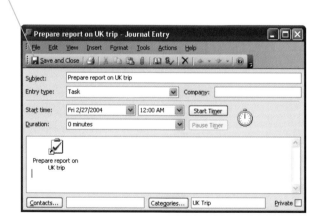

You must select one of the 20 Outlook entry types provided (Outlook does not allow you to create additional types).

4 To track an external (non-Outlook) event, open the Journal and click the New Journal Entry button. Specify the entry type, subject, contact, time, and any other details you have available.

When to Journal

The way you use the Journal depends on the type of projects you undertake, and the extent to which other people or other organizations are involved.

Journal entries may supplement the normal methods of tracking progress through the Outlook folders, by collecting information on specific types of activity or by concentrating on a certain contact. Such records will be useful for billable work, as an audit trail to support your charges, or to provide evidence when you need to challenge an invoice.

Another approach to the Journal is to allow it to capture all activities. You would not expect to review the data on a regular basis, but you could use it to analyze the overall activity, or to investigate issues such as how much time or attention you have devoted to a particular topic.

However, to a large extent, Outlook encourages you to leave the Journal switched off. You can, for example, track activities by contact name without using the Journal. See page 140.

To see the details recorded for a particular contact:

Locate the entry in the Contacts folder, and double-click to open it. Select the Activities tab, and the list of activities relevant to that contact will be shown.

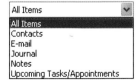

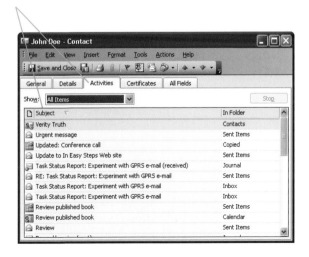

Contact activities

To track tasks, appointments, e-mail, notes, or documents related to a contact without using the Journal, specify the contact when you create Outlook items. You can also link existing Outlook items and add the contact details.

To link a new item to a contact:

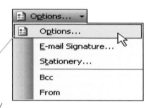

1 When you are composing an e-mail message, click Options (or click the down arrow and select Options). Specify the Contacts and the Categories associated with the message.

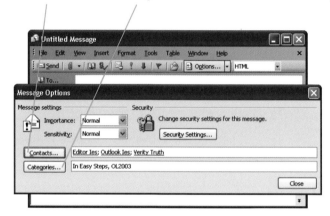

2 Some of the Outlook items, such as Appointments and Tasks, have the Contacts field and button displayed on the input form.

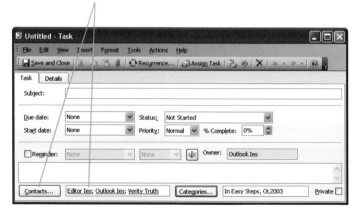

You can link a new contact to an Outlook item or Office document that has already been created, without having to open the item.

To link an Outlook item to a new contact:

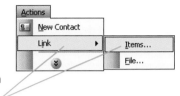

3 Create or Open the contact to which you want to link items, and select Actions, Link, Items, to open the Link Items to Contacts panel.

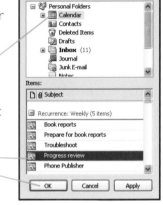

4 From the Look in box, pick the folder that contains the Outlook item or items to be linked with the contact.

Repeat these steps for each of the folders that contain relevant items.

5 From the Items list, select the specific items that you want to link to the contact and click OK.

To link a document to a new contact:

6 Select Actions, Link, File and in the Choose file box, locate and select the file you want to link to the contact, then click Insert.

This will generate a Journal entry. Click Save and Close to add the entry to the Journal. Note that you can only add one file at a time.

7 From the contact record, click the Activities tab to see the links that will have been set up.

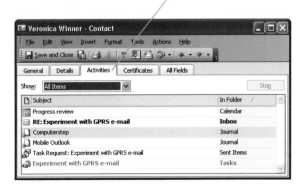

Outlook Notes

If messages, reminders and Journal entries are not enough, you can always write yourself a Note. Outlook Notes are the PC equivalent of the ubiquitous sticky notes, and even come in a variety of colors, yellow included. Notes can contain memory joggers, phone numbers, names or anything that you want to make a point of remembering. They are saved in the Notes folder, and you can also leave notes open on the screen. To create a note:

1 Click the down-arrow next to the New button, and select Note.

2 Type the text of the note. The text will be used as the title for the note. If you press Enter, the text you typed before pressing the first Enter is used.

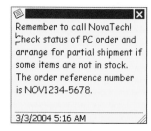

3 Select Notes from the Navigation Pane, or press Ctrl+5 to display the Notes folder.

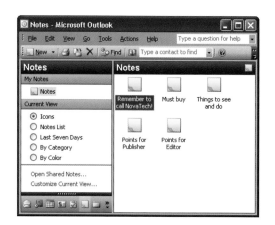

Your notes appear as icons in the folder, with the title used as the icon name. Long icon names will be abbreviated.

Working with Notes

To make sure that you remember some fact or action for tomorrow, you can add a note to the desktop.

Another way to make sure that you see the note is to set up Outlook to start with the Notes folder open (see page 146).

1   Left-click the note, drag it onto the desktop and release the mouse button at a suitable position.

2   The note is stored on the desktop as a .msg file. A copy remains in the Notes folder.

Double-click the icon on the desktop to open the note without starting the full Outlook.

3   Whenever you see the desktop, for example when you restart the system, you'll see the note.

Notes are created in a standard window which you can move, re-size or overlay with other windows. Each open note has a Taskbar entry.

Edit the text in the open note to add to, or change the contents. All the changes are also written to the note in the folder. There is no need to save the contents. You can change the size of the note by dragging an edge or a corner, and you can move the note around the screen by clicking and dragging the title heading.

To see a list of other actions you can perform on the open note:

You can choose one of five background colors for the note. Copy and paste functions are also supported, though for unformatted text only.

4   Left-click the Control menu button on the Note window to display the list of commands that are available, and choose a function, e.g. Color.

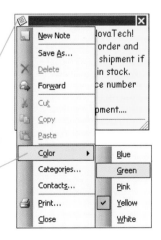

Note settings

As well as changing the style of individual notes, you can specify the color, size, and fonts to use for new notes. The changes apply to new notes only. Existing notes will not be affected.

To view or change the settings for new Notes:

1 Select Tools from the Menu bar, click Options, click the Preferences tab and choose Note Options.

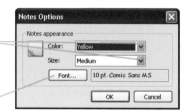

2 Click the down-arrows to choose the background color and the initial size for new notes. The defaults are Yellow and Medium.

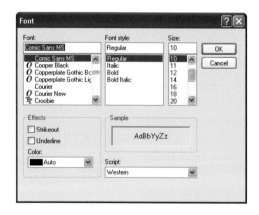

3 Check the font settings. You can use any of the Windows fonts and styles. The selection applies to the whole note and it can't be changed for existing notes.

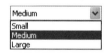

Create a new note, and copy/paste from the old note, if you want to display it in a different font.

When you choose to show or hide the time and date on notes, the changes applies immediately on all notes, including any open notes.

Advanced Options...

4 Click Tools, Options, Other tab, and select Advanced Options. Clear or check the box to hide or show the date and time on notes.

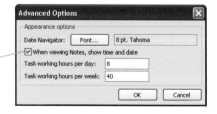

Viewing Notes

You can organize the way the Notes folder is arranged, using the View options.

1 Open the Notes folder and select a view from the Navigation Pane, or click View, Arrange By, Current View, and choose a view.

2 The Icons view shows the notes as large icons, with their contents as their names.

3 Click Small Icons, to show the notes in a list style, with small icons.

4 Select the Note List view, to show the notes in tabular form, with the title, creation date and category for each note.

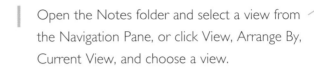

5 Select View, AutoPreview to show the Note List format plus the first three lines of each note (or whole note, if no more than three lines).

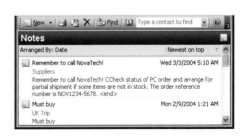

Starting up with Notes

*Check your notes
every time you
start Outlook, so
you can check for
action items.*

1 Click Tools, Options, select
the Other tab and click the
Advanced Options button.

2 You can choose to start up in any of the Outlook folders: Today,
Inbox, Calendar, etc. Choose the Notes folder.

Add a note for yourself or the next Outlook user, on screen and in
the Notes folder. This uses a shortcut to Outlook with the
appropriate startup parameter (see page 28).

3 Find Outlook.exe and create a
Windows Desktop shortcut.

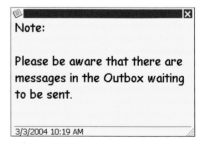

*Leave a note for
yourself or the
next user, without
having to load up
the full Outlook*

application.

4 Right-click the shortcut
and select Properties.

5 Add this parameter to
the Target box:
/c ipm.stickynote

6 Double-click the modified
shortcut, and start up with a
blank note sheet.

*If you've set
Outlook to open
in the Notes
folder, as shown
above, you can*

close the message and it will be
displayed the next time Outlook
starts up.

7 Type your message and leave
it on the screen. There will
also be a copy of the note in
the Notes folder.

Note:

**Please be aware that there are
messages in the Outbox waiting
to be sent.**

3/3/2004 10:19 AM

Mobile Outlook

The more you get used to the extended facilities in Outlook, the more you'll miss them when you are working away from the office. You can create printouts of the relevant information from your folders or, with the right types of electronic companions, you can take Outlook along with you on your trip.

Covers

Chapter Nine

Planning a trip

You can e-mail the offices and the hotels that you are going to visit. Use your calendar to record the itinerary for your journey, as well as the meetings and activities that you'll take part in when you arrive. Prepare to-do lists and agendas, and collate background information and prompts. Obtain names, telephone numbers and personal details of those you are meeting, from your contacts list.

The wide range of functions in Outlook 2003 come into their own when you are planning a trip. As well as all the standard PIM (Personal Information Management) support, it can even help you generate location maps and driving directions.

When planning a trip to a different country or different time zone, it's helpful to show both time zones on your calendar.

1 Select Calendar, Options, Preferences, and click Calendar Options. Then click Time Zone in the Advanced Options.

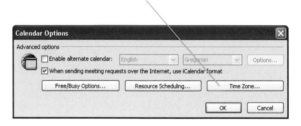

Don't change the setting for your primary time zone, or you will upset the values for all-day events – the nominal end time of 12pm will be altered to shorten or lengthen the day.

2 Select Show an additional time zone, and select your planned destination.

3 Adjust for daylight saving time, so that you display the actual time at the location.

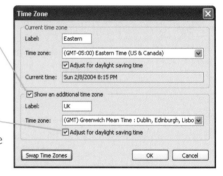

The dual time zones will only appear in the Day or Working Week views. The primary time will be displayed in the other views.

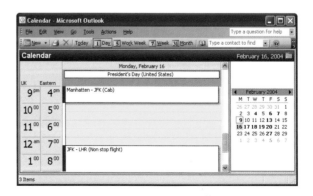

To allow the whole day to display, select Customize Current View, click Other Settings and set Time Scale to the maximum interval of 60 minutes. You can then see

how events can extend into another day, in one of the time zones.

4 Complete the entries in your Calendar for the period of your trip, using the second time zone to help convert local times.

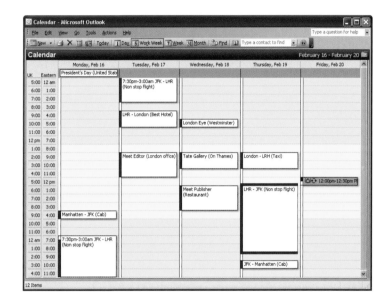

If you use Outlook to create meeting requests, manage tasks or journal activities, there could be large amounts of data related to your trip, already stored in your Outlook folders.

5 Open Tasks and define activities related to your trip, or open Notes to give yourself useful reminders.

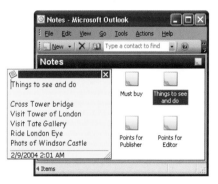

When you have all the details for your trip set up in your Outlook folders, you need to tackle the problem of accessing that information while you are on the road, or in the air.

6 Your Outlook records may contain other relevant information, for example, messages and attachments connected with the trip. Specify a category such as UK Trip for all related Outlook items.

Printing your folders

You can print individual items, or a view of all the items in an Outlook folder. There are various predefined print styles, suited to particular types of data, views, or paper sizes. For example, to print your notes for the trip:

1 Open Notes, set the Current View to Notes List, select Customize Current View and click Filter, More Choices. Specify Categories, e.g. UK Trip, and click OK.

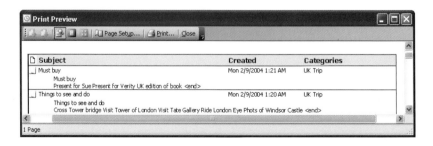

2 Select File, Print Preview, and you'll see the notes with the full content, in tabular form, with multiple entries per page. Click the Print button to make a copy.

...cont'd

Outlook provides five different print styles for Contacts data, ranging from address card to phone directory.

3 To print an address book for the trip, open Contacts, and set the Current View to Address Cards. Customize the current view to show contacts for the UK Trip category. Then click File, Print.

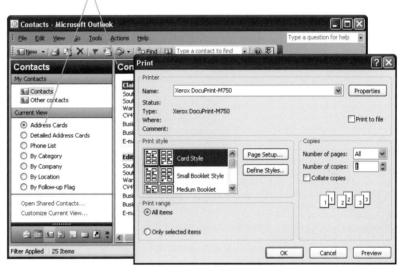

4 Select Tools from the Menu bar then select Find, Advanced Find.

5 Choose Any type of Outlook item, click Browse to choose the folders, click More Choices and specify the Categories, and then click Find Now to list the items.

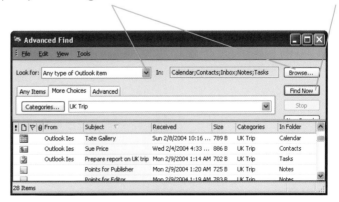

Laptop Outlook

If you use a laptop PC for Outlook, you can take it with you and work offline with your Outlook folders. This will give you access to all your information, and you can make changes to your schedule, your contacts or your notes.

Taking a laptop PC along, you'll be able to work with all your Outlook folders. If you have the chance to connect to the Internet, you'll be able to collect and send e-mail. To reduce dialup costs however, you may want to minimize the time it takes to download.

1   To change your download options, select Tools, Send/Receive, Send/Receive Settings, Define Send/Receive Groups.

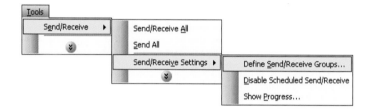

If you run Outlook on a desktop PC, you can copy the Outlook folders onto a laptop PC to use while you are traveling. Make sure that you specify to leave messages at the server (see page 98), so that you can download them to your desktop PC when you return to the office.

☑ Leave a copy of messages on the server

2   Select All Accounts (or the appropriate group, if you have defined others - see page 87) and click the Edit button.

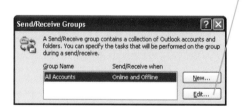

3   Choose to download headers only. Note that you have the alternative option to restrict the size of downloads.

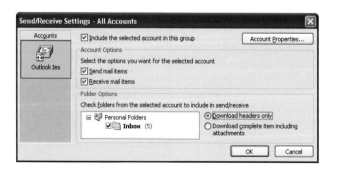

...cont'd

As soon as you have finished the download, you can disconnect and work offline to review and mark up the message headers.

4 When you click Send/Receive, only the header details for the messages will be downloaded, but the full size will be shown.

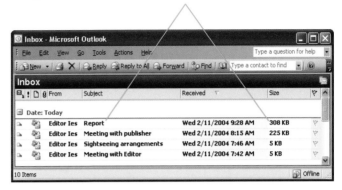

5 Right-click a message header in the Inbox, and mark the messages that you want to downloaded later.

Note that if you delete a message on the laptop, it will be deleted from the server also, the next time you select Send/Receive.

6 The next time that you press Send/Receive, the full contents of any marked messages, plus any new message headers will be downloaded from the server.

With e-mail systems based on Exchange Server, where the Outlook folders are stored at the server, you may be able to connect remotely to your server, and access your e-mail even when you are away from the office.

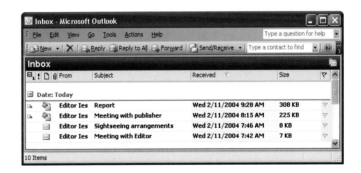

7 When you return to the office, redisplay the Send/Receive settings and change to download complete items, if your laptop PC is also your main system.

Windows Mobile 2003

Mobile, hand-held systems are designed for ease of connection to networks and to your desktop PC, and can synchronize PIM data including messages, contacts, calendars and tasks.

Before you can connect your mobile device to your desktop PC, you must install Microsoft ActiveSync on the desktop PC. There should be a version on the CD provided with your mobile device, but you can find the latest version at the Microsoft Web site.

1 Visit http://www.microsoft.com/windowsmobile/default.mspx, type ActiveSync in the search field and click Go.

2 Follow the link for the download of the latest version of Microsoft ActiveSync. This is a 4MB file named Msasync.exe.

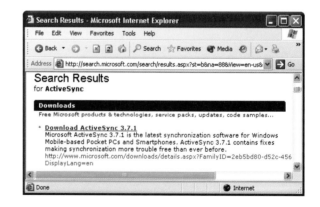

This application is intended for use with a variety of different types of Pocket PCs and Smartphones, but in all cases, you must

You must not attach the Pocket PC cradle to your desktop PC, until ActiveSync has been installed and activated.

ActiveSync will require about 10MB disk space on the hard drive of your desktop PC. Some additional space will also be required to keep track of the settings for the device synchronization.

When you attach your device to your PC and click Next, ActiveSync will scan your ports and automatically detect the device, whether it is a Pocket PC (see page 156), a Smartphone (see page 159) or a combination (see page 161).

start off by installing ActiveSync on your desktop PC, before you attempt to connect the particular device.

3 Double-click the downloaded file to begin the installation of ActiveSync. The wizard guides you through the stages.

4 Click Next, and accept the suggested folder (or choose an alterative location) and ActiveSync installs and starts up.

5 If you are not ready to proceed immediately, click Cancel and you can run ActiveSync later from the Start menu.

Pocket PC

A typical Pocket PC, the HP iPAQ h4150, is a small, light device with a 3½" (240 x 320) color touch screen and a 400 MHz processor. Pocket PC versions of Outlook, Word, Excel and Internet Explorer are included. It has wireless connections for networks and devices, e.g. phones or printers. A cradle with a USB port connects it to your desktop PC, so you can set up a partnership to synchronize Outlook folders and files.

Choose Standard Partnership to connect to your own desktop PC, and Guest Partnership for times when you need to set up a temporary connection on another PC.

If you use Exchange Server, you can also synchronize directly with the server.

1. Start ActiveSync, if it is not already running, and then attach the Pocket PC and its cradle to the USB port on the PC.

2. ActiveSync will recognize your device, and set up a partnership between the two machines.

Scroll down to see the remaining entries. Note that you may be offered some items such as Pocket Access which only exist on the desktop PC. If you select such items, they'll be ignored during synchronization.

3. ActiveSync lists the data sources that are available, and preselects Calendar, Contacts, Favorites, Inbox, and also Tasks.

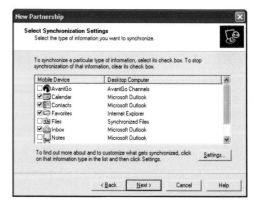

ActiveSync compares the contents of the Pocket PC and the desktop PC, looking for changes in folder structures and file contents, It counts how many items are not synchronized, then brings the two systems into line. Where there are existing items on the Pocket PC, you can choose to merge or replace them.

4 Add any others you need, for example Notes, then click Next for ActiveSync to complete the setup and begin the synchronization.

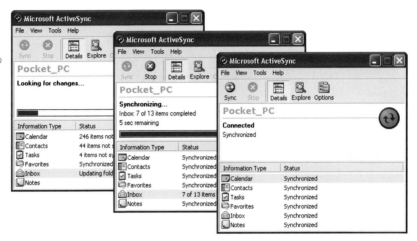

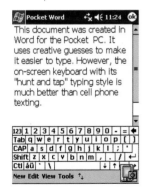

You can create a document in Pocket Word (using the on-screen keyboard), and it will be stored in the Pocket-PC My Documents folder, and synchronized to the desktop PC when you connect.

5 If you choose Files, it adds a copy of the Pocket-PC My Documents folder to your desktop PC, where you can store files that will be shared between two devices.

Working with the Pocket PC

If you are working in a different time zone, click the date on the Today screen, and set the Visiting time zone. Then your calendar will show the local times for your appointments.

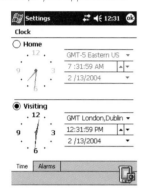

1 When you work with your Pocket PC after synchronizing, you'll find that calendar entries, contacts, tasks and notes have been added.

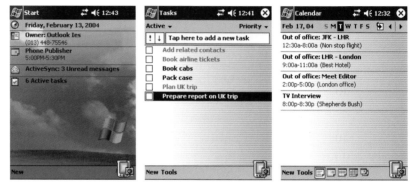

2 You can deal with your Outlook items, e.g. update entries, mark tasks as complete or create new entries. The changes will be applied the next time you connect to the desktop PC.

With the network and Bluetooth connections, you may be able to access the Internet and update your e-mail while you are away from the office, for example, at an Internet coffee shop that offers wireless connections.

You may make changes to Outlook items or files on the Pocket PC, and find on your return that these have also been changed on the desktop PC. ActiveSync recognizes this and warns you.

3 When two items appear to be in conflict, ActiveSync marks them as unresolved.

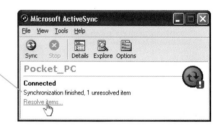

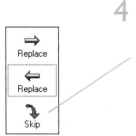

4 You can accept one or other as the true version, skip the items, or leave the two versions unreconciled and examine them later.

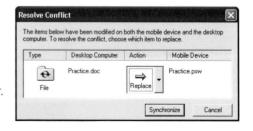

Smartphone

The SPV E200 is a tri-band GSM/GPRS cell phone which includes vibrating call alert, polyphonic ringtones, voice dialing, voice recording, MP3 player, speakerphone as well as WAP for Internet connection.

The SPV E200 Smartphone from Orange is so named because it offers Sound Pictures and Video. It runs the Smartphone version of Windows Mobile 2003. The 1¾" (176 x 220) display and the 132 MHz processor are lower spec than the Pocket PC, but this device uses keys rather than a touch display, and it features both Bluetooth and a digital camera. It also includes Pocket Outlook, plus lots of other software including Pocket Internet Explorer, MSN Messenger, Windows Media Player and Voice Notes manager. And, you can create a partnership with your desktop PC.

1 Install ActiveSync and start it, so it waits for your device to connect (see page 155). If you've already defined a partnership, you'll need to select File, Get Connected, to put ActiveSync into the waiting state.

Follow the same steps as for the Pocket PC, to select the Standard Partnership and synchronize with the desktop PC.

However, you'll be offered a much shorter list of options, since the Smartphone edition doesn't support Office applications.

2 Connect the Smartphone and cradle to the desktop PC, to set up a partnership to synchronize Calendar, Contacts, Inbox and Tasks.

3 Appointments, Contacts, Messages and Tasks are stored on your Smartphone.

The SPV E200 doesn't have a Visiting time zone, so you have to set the main time zone to your current destination. Then it will show messages with local times.

With Bluetooth, WAP, and always-on connection to the Internet, you can update your e-mail while you are away from the office, especially if you use Exchange Server e-mail.

You can transfer files between the desktop PC and the Smartphone, since ActiveSync allows you to explore the folders on the Smartphone, which appears as a Mobile Device in My Computer. Make a copy of the Smartphone My Documents folder on your desktop PC, and keep it in sync manually.

1 The Smartphone has a Today interface which includes access to Calendar and Mail – MMS (multimedia), SMS (text) and Inbox.

2 Click Start to display the command list for Contacts and for Tasks (on the second page). There are lots of commands, but you won't find Word or Excel or even Outlook Notes. Also there's no general file synchronization.

3 Click Explore in ActiveSync, and navigate through Mobile Device, My Smartphone, Storage. Here you'll find Smartphone's My Documents, where you can save, copy or delete files that are stored on the Smartphone.

Pocket PC Phone

The O2 XDA II looks like a Pocket PC, with its 3½", 240 x 320 color touch screen, the 400 MHz processor and the Bluetooth support. Pocket PC versions of Outlook, Word, Excel and Internet Explorer are included. And there's a cradle with a USB port, to connect to your desktop PC. But the software is the Phone edition, and the XDA II is a tri-band cell phone, which offers GSM and always-on GPRS network connection. And let's not forget the built-in digital camera. With a product this good there has to be a catch – the XDA II is currently available in Europe and the Far East only, although it does function in the USA and worldwide.

1 Install and start ActiveSync to wait for you to connect the XDA II, or select File, Get Connected, if you already have devices defined.

2 Connect the XDA II and cradle to the desktop PC, to set up a partnership. When setup completes, ActiveSync matches the Calendar, Contacts, Inbox, Notes and Task items, then sets up a new folder to allow data files to be synchronized.

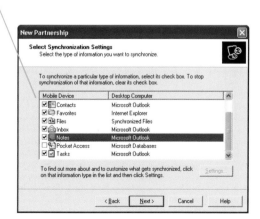

Pocket_PC My Documents   O2_XDA_II My Documents

1 When you check your Pocket PC phone after synchronizing, you'll find your calendar entries, contacts, tasks and notes added.

You can set a visiting time zone for the Pocket PC Phone device, and process your Outlook folders offline.

You can also define your e-mail account details and connect to the e-mail server while you are away from the office, using the Web Mobile GPRS service.

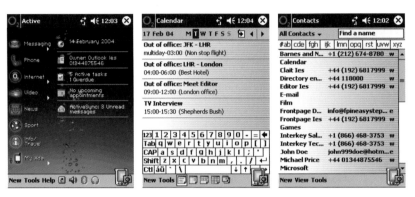

2 Away from the office, your new mail is detected and downloaded into an Inbox associated with your e-mail account, and separate from the ActiveSync Inbox.

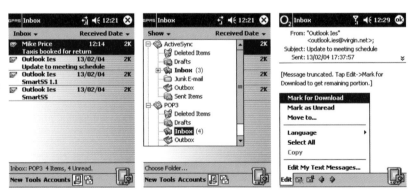

Only copies of the messages are downloaded, and they remain on the server to be downloaded to your main e-mail system on your desktop PC, and copied during synchronization to your ActiveSync Inbox.

3 When you open a mail item, you just see the header. You can mark the message for download the next time you connect via the Web GPRS service, when you can also send replies.

Of course, you'll also have all the power of the cell phone network and can send multimedia and text messages, make voice calls and keep a photographic record of your trip.

Business Contact Manager

Outlook 2003 with Business Contact Manager is a single-user desktop application designed to meet the needs of small businesses with fewer than 25 employees. It helps manage business contacts and opportunities, track sales activities, and analyze sales performance.

Covers

Chapter Ten

About Business Contact Manager

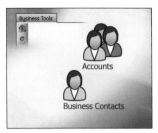

If you deal with customers and potential customers and have to manage sales prospects, you may find yourself searching through index cards, sticky notes and bits of paper to find records of conversations. The problem with jotting down details such as customer names, or purchase requirements is that it is very easy to lose or misread the information.

If you start off with BCM and decide to upgrade later, you'll be able to migrate your customer data from BCM to Microsoft CRM.

The answer may be Business Contact Manager (BCM) which is a single-user COM add-in for Outlook 2003 that provides additional features for tracking contact activity and sales opportunities. BCM is available on a separate CD in Office 2003 Professional Edition, and in Office 2003 Small Business Edition. It is not available as a stand-alone product.

BCM provides a center for storing the information, and makes it easy to reference and use. You'll also benefit when you need to make reports or plan your sales activities.

Being a single-user desktop program, BCM stores data on your PC and is not designed to share the customer contact information with other users. It assumes that, if there are several people dealing with customers, each will have a separate territory that is individually managed. If you do find the need to share business contact data with others, you may need a multi-user Customer Relationship Management product such as Microsoft CRM, which is designed for companies with a staff of 25 to 200.

Microsoft
Business
Solutions

Install Business Contact Manger

The requirements for Business Contact Manger include and exceed the requirements for Outlook 2003, as detailed on page 12.

System requirements

Outlook with Business Contact Manager must be used in combination with a POP3, IMAP or HTML e-mail Server. It is not enabled when used in combination with Exchange Server or Microsoft Small Business Server configured for MAPI based e-mail. The hardware and software requirements for BCM include:

- Pentium III 450 MHz or higher processor recommended

- 256 MB memory or above

- Windows 2000 SP3 or Windows XP, or later

- 190 MB available hard-disk space

- CD-ROM drive

- SVGA 800 x 600 resolution monitor with 256 colors, or higher

- Mouse or pointing device

There is an Outlook 2003 update on the Microsoft Office Update Web site which will allow you to use Windows Small Business Server to run BCM.

Running Setup

If Outlook is running when you insert the CD, you'll get an error message saying that you should close Outlook before continuing.

1 Close Outlook, and insert the CD containing BCM. The Setup program will automatically start.

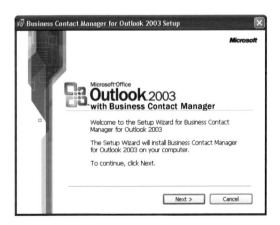

If you'd changed the program folder during the installation of Office 2003, you should apply an equivalent change at this stage also.

2 Click Next to continue and accept the terms in the license agreement, and the suggested Program Files folder.

Setup wizard

The Setup Wizard copies the required files and installs the new services required for BCM. You won't be asked for a CD code or to activate the program, since you are already licensed for Outlook 2003.

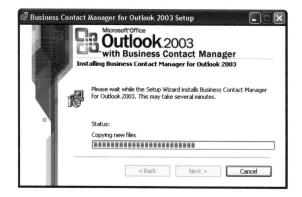

1 Click Finish when the Setup Wizard completes. There's no need to restart the PC.

2 Restart Outlook and you'll be asked if you wish to use BCM with your current Outlook profile. Click Yes to confirm.

When you click Yes, BCM will initialize the database ready for use.

BCM uses the Microsoft SQL Server Desktop Engine (MSDE), a run-time database engine that provides the core features of SQL Server without the need to install SQL Server.

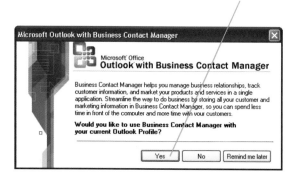

3 Click File, Help, and you'll find a list of new options related to the use of BCM. These are:

- BCM Help
- BCM Quick Start Guide
- BCM Tours
- About BCM

Exploring BCM

When you install BCM, the Outlook menus and toolbars are extended to include BCM features, and the BCM folders are added to the Folders list.

When BCM is installed, the Outlook menus are modified to include additional commands, and the Business Contact Manager toolbar appears by default below the Outlook toolbar.

The BCM toolbar is not added to the View, Toolbars menu but you can hide or display the toolbar by selecting Tools, Customize, and clicking the Toolbars tab.

The File, New menu is extended to allow you to create new items for the BCM database.

The new Business Tools menu lets you display database records and related items, generate reports, access your product list, connect to business services, and manage e-mail linking preferences.

2 The File, Business Database command opens a wizard to help you import or export data, and maintain the database.

3 The File, Import and Export command is divided into two parts: Outlook and BCM.

4 There are extra entries on the Go menu for BCM folders (but no keyboard shortcuts).

Business contacts

The BCM contact details are similar to those in Outlook but have additional details, including financial status and preferred method of contact.

Although a contact record may show a preferred method of contact, this is for information only - Outlook does not take note of the preference when you are sending messages.

If you save your business contact information using another program such as ACT!, Excel, QuickBooks, or any application that can create a .csv file, you can import that data into BCM using the wizard.

These composite views summarize the steps in the processes. The Import and Export wizard is shown in fuller detail on pages 68-69.

To export your existing business contacts information and import it to BCM:

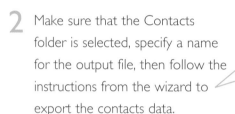

1 Select File, Import and Export, then Outlook. Choose Export to a file, and specify the file type Comma Separated Values (Windows).

2 Make sure that the Contacts folder is selected, specify a name for the output file, then follow the instructions from the wizard to export the contacts data.

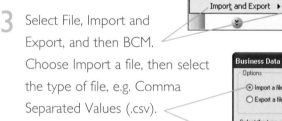

3 Select File, Import and Export, and then BCM. Choose Import a file, then select the type of file, e.g. Comma Separated Values (.csv).

4 Browse to select the file with the exported information, then select BCM's Business Contacts folder as the destination. Choose whether to allow duplicates. Click Map, to match the input to the database. This is needed the first time you import, but the mapping becomes the default for subsequent imports.

...cont'd

5 Drag field names from the CSV list and drop them onto their matching entries on the Business Contacts list.

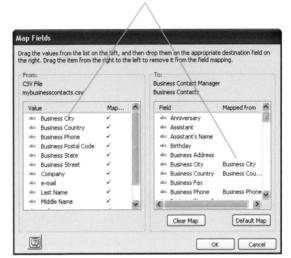

Since the lists are quite long, it may be easier to select the source field: press Ctrl+L, then locate and select the target field and press Ctrl+L again.

6 Complete the steps in the wizard to import the data.

You can copy contacts directly between Outlook Contacts and the BCM Business Contacts, when there are relatively few contacts to transfer.

When you drag and drop from Outlook Contacts to BCM Business Contacts, the item is moved. Hold down the Ctrl key before releasing the mouse button, and the item will be copied instead.

When you drag and drop from BCM Business Contacts to Outlook Contacts, items are always copied, not moved.

7 Display the Folder List. Select the contact that you want to add and drag it to the Business Contacts folder in BCM, then release the mouse button.

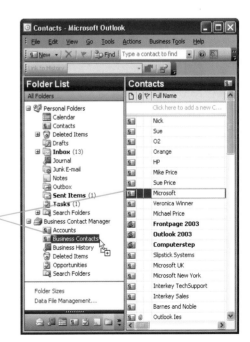

Create an account

The BCM account record is broadly equivalent to a customer record, though you may have more than one account per customer.

1 Click the arrow on the New button and select Account, or select Accounts from the Folder List or Business Tools, to open the folder. Double-click where indicated to create a new account.

To select the primary contact from the BCM Business Contacts folder, click this button:

2 Specify the details for the account, including account name, primary contact, business address, business phone numbers, e-mail address and Web page address.

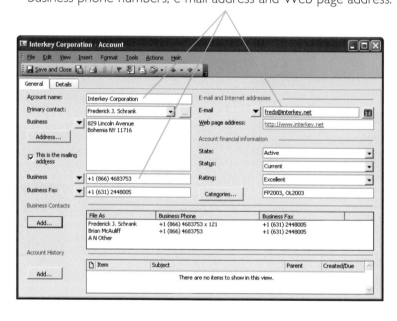

To add further contacts, click Add, Add Existing Contact and select them from the BCM Business Contacts folder, or click Create New Contact and type the name.

3 Specify account financial information if appropriate, selecting from the list of options provided, to define the:

- Rating
- Status
- State

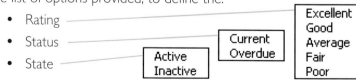

4 The only mandatory data for the account record is the name.

Specify an opportunity

The way you use the Opportunity record depends on the type of business or service that you run. Opportunities may be linked to Contacts or to Accounts, and could include product details.

1 Select Opportunity from the New button, or open the Opportunities folder and double click inside, to display the Opportunity record form.

2 Enter the details for the prospect, providing a title, linking it to an account or a business contact, and setting a success probability.

To select the associated account from the Accounts folder, or the contact from the Business Contacts folder, click this button:

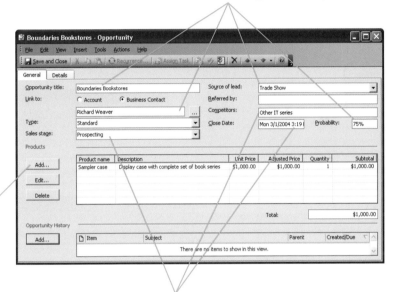

Add product details to the opportunity if this information is available. You can select entries from the BCM product list (see page 172), or simply type in the details.

3 Name possible competitors for the business, confirm or adjust the closing date and select characteristics from the lists:

- Source of lead
- Sales stage
- Type

Standard
Bulk Order
Delivery
Special Order

Prospecting
Qualification
Needs Analysis
Proposal/Price Quote
Negotiation/Review
Closed Won
Closed Lost

Advertisement
Direct Mail
Employee Referral
External Referral
Partner
Public Relations
Seminar
Trade Show
Web
Word-of-Mouth
Other

4 The Opportunity cannot be saved until you link it to an account or contact record.

Product lists

The master product list is a very simple listing, which can be created manually or by importing data.

BCM maintains a Product Master List of the product information that you import or enter when defining business opportunities (see page 171).

To add a product to the list:

Select an existing entry and you can click Edit to make changes to the contents, or click
Delete to remove the entry completely.

Add...

Edit...

Delete

1. Select Business Tools, Product List to display the current list of products, and click Add to create a new entry.

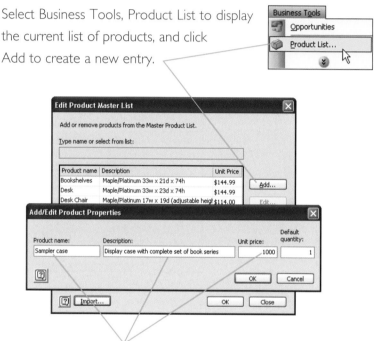

The imported file must be in .csv format without field headings, and must include:
Product Name, Description, Unit Price, Default Quantity. The data should not include quote marks, or currency symbols or thousand separators e.g. put 1000 rather than 1,000.

2. Type the Product name, the Description and the unit price (do not include the currency symbol), then click OK to add it.

3. Click Import to add data from an external source. You can amend the existing list, or replace it.

Reporting

1 Select Business Tools from the Menu bar and click Reports to list the groups.

2 Click each group in turn to see the list of reports offered:
- Business Contacts
- Accounts
- Opportunities
- Other

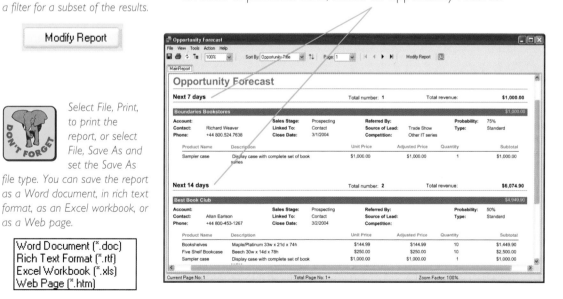

Modify Report

3 For example, select Opportunity Forecast to see a week-by-week forecast of potential sales, based on opportunity records.

Word Document (*.doc)
Rich Text Format (*.rtf)
Excel Workbook (*.xls)
Web Page (*.htm)

Business services

BCM can be used with the bCentral Services to set up direct e-mail with your customers, if you export your business contacts to bCentral List Builder. You could also expand your e-mailing list using the bCentral iSales Leads.

While connected to the Internet, select Business Tools, and click Business Services to access the bCentral Services Web site.

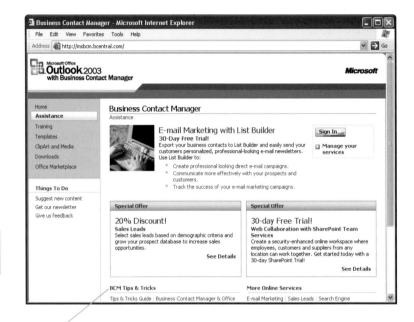

BCM offers specialized content for other regions and countries. Click the link at the foot of the page to see the worldwide list.

Your current setting is: United States

Business Contact Manager Worldwide

To download one of the documents, right-click the link and select Save Target As, then specify the file name and folder.

2 Click the BCM Tips & Tricks link to download documents giving you useful tips for using BCM with Office 2003 applications.

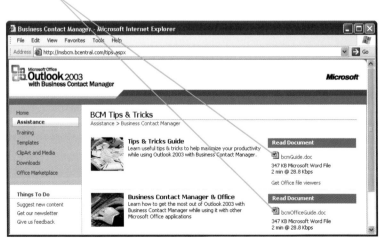

Managing Security

You need to keep your data and definitions safe from harm, either accidental or deliberate, and you must be able to recover in the situations where problems do arise. Outlook 2003 provides the tools and facilities you need.

Covers

Chapter Eleven

Managing data

Outlook items are stored in the file Outlook.pst, your personal folder file. You can create additional personal folders to help manage your data, perhaps keeping data for a particular project in a separate personal folder. Extra personal folders are also used for backup and for archiving, or for sharing information with other users, on a shared drive, or by sending a copy over the Internet.

If you are using Exchange Server, your messages, calendar, and other Outlook items, are stored centrally on the server, although you can also use PST files on your local hard disk.

The default file and display names for .pst files are set as Personal Folders(1), Personal Folders (2) etc. but the purposes of the folders will be more obvious if you assign meaningful names.

To add a Personal Folder:

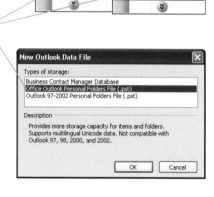

1. Select File, New, Outlook Data File, and choose Office Outlook file (unless you'll be accessing this folder using older versions of Outlook).

2. Specify the file name, e.g. MyProject.pst and then specify the display name e.g. MyProject.

3. The new Personal Folder will be displayed in the Folders List. Initially there will be no subfolders, other than the defaults Deleted Items and Search Folders.

4. Create new subfolders (see page 95), and drag and drop or move items from your default personal folder to the new folder.

Archiving

There may be data, such as copies of sent e-mails, that you want to retain but don't need online all the time. You can use the AutoArchive feature in Outlook to move these items to another folder.

To set up a folder to automatically archive using the default AutoArchive settings:

1 Right-click one of the folders in the Folder List, select Properties, then click the AutoArchive tab.

By default, Outlook starts AutoArchive every 14 days and archives items older than six months, putting them in the Archive.pst personal folders file. You can choose not to archive a particular folder, or can specify custom AutoArchive settings.

2 Select "Archive items in this folder using the default settings", then click OK.

3 Repeat for each folder that you want to archive, or click Default Archive Settings and choose "Apply these settings to all folders now".

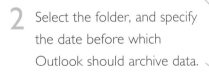

You can archive data on demand, for example, when you want to transfer records to a new PC, or just before you synchronize your Pocket PC.

Archive data manually

1 Select File, Archive and choose "Archive this folder and all subfolders".

2 Select the folder, and specify the date before which Outlook should archive data.

3 Click Browse to specify the folder and the file name for the archive, or type the path and file name, then click OK.

Backup and recovery

It is wise to make a regular backup of the data on your hard disk, in case your system fails. There are several ways to backup Outlook data,

- Backup the drive – use a program such as the Windows Backup Utility to backup the hard drive

The first two methods involve saving and restoring copies of the Outlook files. This will bring your system back to the position when the backup was made.

- Backup the files – copy the .pst file and other Outlook related files to a different hard disk

- Backup the Outlook items – export copies of selected folders to a backup .pst file

To identify the files required for Outlook:

1. Select File, Data File Management to show the files being used by Outlook.

By default, the files that Outlook uses are stored in the Documents and Settings area for the user. The Outlook configuration files are in C:\Documents and Settings\User\Application Data\Microsoft\Outlook.

2. Select one of the files and click Open Folder.

The Outlook data files are in: C:\Documents and Settings\User\Local Settings\Application Data\Microsoft\Business Contact Manager\Outlook.

In these folder paths, User represents the user name e.g. Michael.

3. Note the path and folder name and make sure this is included in your backup.

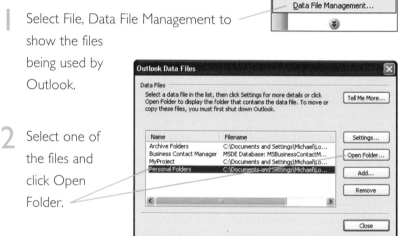

4. The BCM database files will be stored in a separate folder adjacent to the Outlook folder.

Export and import

The drive and file backup methods copy the whole of the Outlook data. If you want a more selective backup, you can use the Export facility.

BCM data

1   Select File, Import and Export, Business Contact Manager.

You can export account and contact data, but for other data you'd need to copy the whole BCM folder.

2   Select Export a file, choose the file format, name the file and select the folder to copy.

3   Follow the wizard to complete the export of the data.

Outlook data

1   Select File, Import and Export, Outlook.

You can export individual folders and subfolders in a variety of formats including .pst. This is similar to the archive process, but the items that are exported are not removed from the Outlook folders.

2   Select Export to a file, choose the file format, and select the folder to copy.

3   Follow the wizard to name the file, and complete the export of the data.

PST Backup Addin

1 Go to http://www.microsoft.com/office and click the link to Downloads for Office 2003, and then Outlook 2003 Addins.

Personal Folders Backup only backs up .PST files. If you have a Microsoft Exchange Server mailbox, your server mailbox folders are usually backed up regularly by your server administrator.

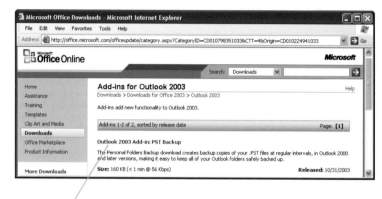

2 Click Outlook 2003 Add-in: PST Backup and click the Download button to transfer the 160 KB pfbackup.exe file.

pfbackup.exe
Win32 Cabinet Self-Extractor
Microsoft Corporation

3 Close Outlook and other Windows applications, and double-click pfbackup.exe to install the Add-in.

4 Start Outlook and select File, Backup to configure the Add-in.

Before you begin the backup process, you might want to check the size of your .pst file. Right-click the top-level folder in Navigation Pane, Folders List, select Properties and click the Folder Size button.

5 Click Options, and choose which personal folders to backup.

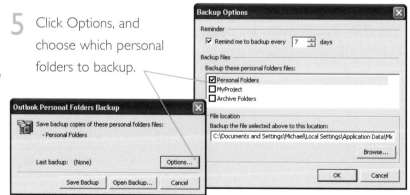

Outlook 2003 Security

Outlook does not make full use of security zones – only the zone selected is taken into account – so there's no point in assigning Web sites to zones.

Outlook 2003 incorporates security features to help protect you from computer viruses and malicious programs, prevent others from stealing your identity, and protect your confidential messages. It will block suspect types of attachments and external images in HTML format messages, support the use of digital signatures and message encryption, and use security zones (as defined in Internet Explorer) to control how HTML format messages are handled.

To view or change the security zone setting:

You are warned that "You are about to change security settings that will affect the way scripts and active content can be run in Microsoft Internet Explorer, Outlook, and any other programs that use security zones." – even if you are just looking!

1 Select Tools, Options and click the Security tab.

2 To view the settings, click the Zone Settings button.

3 Click OK on the warning message.

4 Click Custom Level.

Although there are four zones shown, you can only select the Internet zone settings or the default Restricted sites zones.

The default choice is Restricted sites, which prevents HTML messages from downloading unsigned ActiveX controls or running Java applets etc.

5 Review the settings for your chosen zone.

Blocked images

1 Open an e-mail message with external image references, as indicated by the [X]'s and by the message in the infobar.

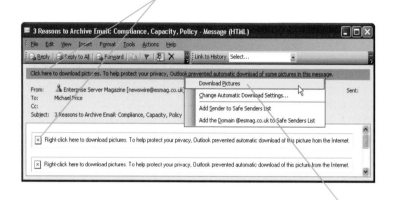

2 Click the message and, if you trust the sender, select Download Pictures to obtain and display the images.

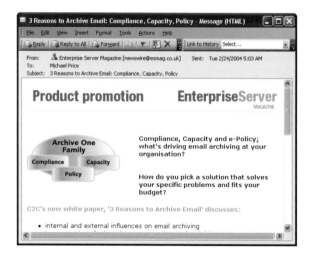

3 Click the message, and select Change Automatic Download Settings to view or amend the settings for HTML messages.

Blocked attachments

When you open an e-mail message with an attachment, you may find that the attachment has been blocked so you cannot save it.

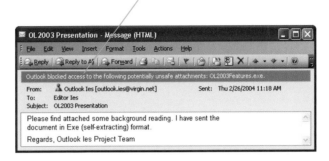

There are two levels of attachment security. Level 1 files types are blocked, while for Level 2 file types, you will be prompted to save the file to your hard disk. Outlook 2003 prevents you from unblocking attachments that are on its Level 1 list.

If you need to send such file types, there are three main options:

- Rename the file to a type not on the list (and tell the recipient)
- Package files using WinZip or equivalent (Zip files are allowed)
- Save the files to a secure server (and send the link in the e-mail)

If you want to receive such files and cannot persuade the sender to take one of the above actions:

- Use a Registry key to allow access to some blocked file types

2 Run Regedit, and locate key HKEY_CURRENT_USER\Software\ Microsoft\Office\11.0\Outlook\Security. Add the string value Level1Remove with a list of file types, separated by semicolons.

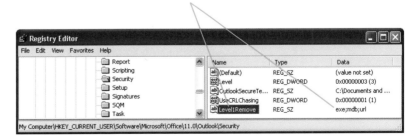

Digital ID and Encryption

To keep your information safe, even when it is being sent over the Internet, you need to encrypt your messages and attachments. To do this requires a Digital ID that confirms your identity.

1 Select Tools, Options and click the Security tab. You can choose to encrypt your e-mail, or to add a digital signature. This will require you to obtain a Digital ID.

2 Click Get A Digital ID, to visit the Office Marketplace where you can find services that issue Digital IDs.

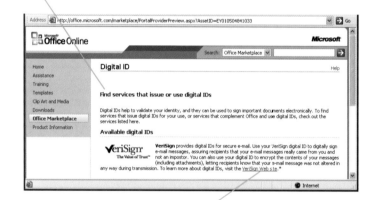

At VeriSign, a personal Digital ID for e-mail is available at a cost of $14.95 for the first year.

There's also a 60-day free trial, if you are unsure about using digital IDs and encryption. Look for the link:

Act Now!
Only $14.95 for a 1yr personal ID

Click here for 60-day free trial

3 Visit the VeriSign Digital ID Center for example, to obtain an e-mail digital certificate. To start, fill in the enrollment form.

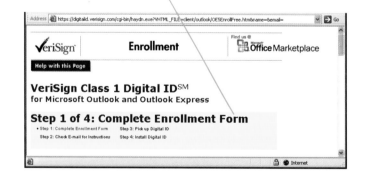

4 VeriSign will send you an e-mail, to validate the e-mail address you provided.

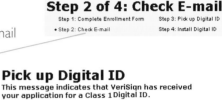

You must use the same browser, on the same PC to enroll, confirm, and install your Digital ID. If you use a different PC for any of the steps, the Digital ID cannot be installed.

5 When the e-mail arrives, click Continue to affirm the address.

Your Certificate Could Not Be Installed

6 The Digital ID will be generated, ready to install into Outlook.

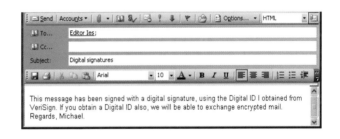

7 When you send a message using the account associated with the Digital ID, you can select "Add digital signature..." (see page 184).

If you and the recipient have exchanged Digital IDs, you will be able to send each other encrypted messages, as well as signed messages.

8 The recipient sees an icon to the right of the headers, indicating that the digital signature is trusted. Click the icon for details.

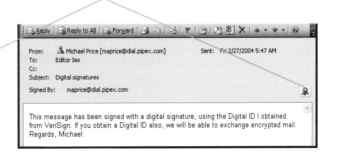

Office Update

1 Select Help, Check for Updates to open the Office Update Web site.

2 Click the link to check for updates, and Office Update will identify the fixes that are needed for your copy of Office.

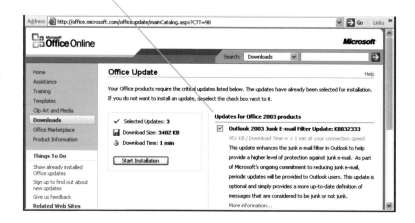

3 If you are facing a problem in Outlook that is not addressed by any of the updates, try searching for "Outlook 2003 hotfixes".

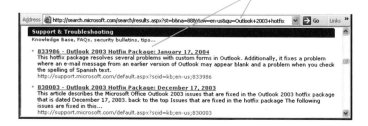

Index

O

U

V

W

X

Y

Z